What People Are Saying About *MySpace Music Marketing*:

"This book on Myspace is so needed and so timely. It's a simple, easy-to-read manual on everything you need to know to get yourself set up on Myspace. Bob knows how to break down complex procedures into easy-to-follow instructions, with some excellent marketing ideas along the way. Kudos once again! –**Gilli Moon**, recording artist, owner of Warrior Girl Music and president of Songsalive!

"Smart, clearly written, and packed with real-world examples, *MySpace Music Marketing* is a true insider's guide to this essential new site."
–**David Battino**, co-author of *The Art of Digital Music*

"Bob's latest book is a thorough guide through the daunting world of MySpace. He provides an honest account of the good, the bad, and the great opportunities that MySpace can bring to indie artists. With the world exploding on the Internet, it's essential for artists to find effective ways to reach new fans. Bob's book is a gold mine of information for new and old MySpacers alike!" –**Kate and Kacey Coppola**

"Bob hits the MySpace nail right on the head. I really appreciated the 49 more places to network the most. He did an entire book on MySpace and then gave us more. That's the kind of detail that sets Bob's stuff light years ahead of everybody else!" –**James Frey**, Blue Island Tribe

"This book covers the how, when, where, why and who of MySpace ... and then launches right into music marketing and band promotion details. Using actual MySpace music marketers in their own words is brilliant and refreshing."
–**Don Harrison**, Baytown Underground

For Pooki. Thanks for turning my space
and your space into Our Space!

Other books and resources by Bob Baker:

Guerrilla Music Marketing Handbook:
201 Self-Promotion Ideas for Songwriters,
Musicians and Bands on a Budget

Guerrilla Music Marketing, Encore Edition:
201 More Self-Promotion Ideas, Tips & Tactics
for Do-It-Yourself Artists

Music Marketing Crash Course: 1,001 Ways to
Promote Yourself, Make Money and Live Your Dreams

Killer Music Press Kits: The 29 Most Important Elements
in Creating Sizzling Music Publicity

For more indie music marketing tips, please visit:
www.TheBuzzFactor.com
www.MusicPromotionBlog.com
www.MusicMarketingBooks.com
And, of course, www.myspace.com/thebuzzfactor

NOTE: This book is not published or endorsed by
MySpace.com or News Corp. Every effort has been made to
ensure the facts and technical ele̶m̶e̶n̶t̶s̶ ̶a̶r̶e̶ ̶a̶c̶c̶u̶r̶a̶t̶e̶.̶ ̶B̶u̶t̶
on the Internet, progress is swift
changed by the time you read th

MySpace Music Marketing

How to Promote & Sell Your Music on the World's Biggest Networking Web Site

Bob Baker

ISBN: 0-9714838-4-1

Published by Spotlight Publications, PO Box 43058,
St. Louis, MO 63143 USA. © 2006 by Bob Baker.

Contents

MySpace.com:
The Big Picture

It's one of the great success stories of the Internet era. Founded by Tom Anderson and Chris DeWolfe in 2003, MySpace.com went from being a new networking site few people had heard of to ranking among the top 5 to 10 most visited web sites in the world — all in two short years!

(To see the most current web site rankings, visit www.alexa.com/site/ds/top_500.)

During one recent week, the only web domains that surfers visited more often than MySpace were Yahoo, Google, Ebay, and the Microsoft Network. That's an impressive feat. And one of the most amazing things is ... most of this growth was fueled by young music fans and independent musicians.

In the same way that younger generations propelled cultural shifts related to Elvis, The Beatles and MTV ... it's teens and twenty-somethings that are driving this latest phenomenon.

What Is MySpace?

MySpace is one of a growing number of "social networking" sites. They work by connecting people. Think of it this way: It's as if each member has his or her own private club of special "friends" who share similar interests. Once you're someone's official friend, you get access to their entire network of friends. And each of those friends has a network of friends.

So, when it comes to social "music networking," if you can get a few excited fans talking about you, word can spread to thousands of people fast!

Avery Storm, a hip-hop and R&B artist based in New York City, described MySpace as the digital version of old-school street marketing. "It's like selling CDs out of your trunk, but it puts the car all over the world," he told writer Mike Grebb in an *Atlas Plugged* article.

Before MySpace, Friendster.com was creating the most buzz in the networking site category. Facebook.com is another popular one aimed at students. But none of them can touch MySpace when it comes to pure numbers.

As of this writing, MySpace can boast:

- Nearly 90 million registered users

- 4 million new users signing up every month (about 135,000 a day)

- More than two million artist and band pages

And it's growing all the time at an astonishing rate!

Who In the Heck Is Tom?

Anyone who has registered with MySpace knows Tom. He's the first friend you automatically get when you set up your profile. Tom's a real guy — with an interesting story ...

In the late 1990s, Tom Anderson was playing in a San Francisco alt-rock band called Swank. The band never made much of a splash, but it made Anderson realize the great void between the most popular major label acts and the least-known artists wallowing in obscurity. Next, he went to film school. A couple of years later he used an online dating site and was impressed by the Internet's potential to connect people whose lives might not otherwise overlap.

Looking to earn some temporary extra cash, Anderson went to work for a start-up tech firm. That's when he met the company's vice president, Chris DeWolfe. By 2001, both had left the firm and went into business together to run a marketing company.

In the spring of 2003, Anderson approached DeWolfe with the idea of creating a cooler social networking site. He wanted it to be a combination of Friendster, Blogger, MP3.com and Craigslist — all rolled into one. The services would be free to members, and money would be made selling ads to companies that wanted to reach these members and the people who visited their pages.

The Unexpected Power Surge

In July of that year, MySpace quietly launched with an initial batch of Los Angeles-based actors, photographers and musicians as its first members. Then, in the fall of 2003 — with no advertising; only word of mouth from users — the site's popularity exploded. And it hasn't slowed down since.

What makes MySpace so different and appealing is that the site gives users a lot of free features and freedom to design and use their pages as they see fit — things that weren't available on many of the other social networking sites. Musical artists can offer streams or downloads of four songs, list all of their upcoming gigs, post photos and videos, publish a blog, list sales links for their CDs and merchandise ... all right from their MySpace page.

And let's not forget your FRIENDS!

When you find someone on MySpace you'd like to get to know better, you send them a request to be added as one of their friends. The person either accepts or declines the request — or never responds at all. Most people accept.

Once you're an official friend, you can post comments

on each other's pages, view each other's complete network of friends, etc. The more friends you have, the more people you potentially have access to — although, as you'll read later, many artists feel the quality of friends you have is more important than the quantity.

The Beauty, the Beast, the Bandwidth

MySpace is a double-edged sword. All of the cool features, and the freedom to use them (to a great extent) as you wish, have helped propel the site's immense popularity. But those same aspects make many pages on the site a bloated mess of oversized images, bandwidth-sucking multimedia files, and ugly font and color choices — not to mention high school level sex talk and titillation.

Still, a growing number of indie bands — including Relient K, My Chemical Romance, Arctic Monkeys, and Hawthorne Heights — claim that MySpace is one of the top factors that led to their success.

Indie acts have profited so much from exposure on the site, guess who came running to join them? You got it: established major label artists. Name any well-known band and you're likely to find a MySpace page either run by them, their management, or their label.

Music has been so hot on the site, the company has launched MySpace Records, a collaboration between MySpace and Interscope Records. It's an indie label that takes advantage of Interscope's distribution channels. Not surprisingly, Tom Anderson is the head of A&R for MySpace Records.

The entertainment industry as a whole has taken note. There are now MySpace pages for TV shows, movies, books and authors, even PETA (People for the Ethical Treatment of Animals) uses MySpace to get the word out by networking with bands and their fans. The site is now catering to the indie film community, hoping to provide a haven for filmmakers in the same way it did for musicians. Also in the works for MySpace: a satellite radio channel and an indie film company.

Ambitious plans!

For an excellent overview of MySpace and how it works, check out this page: http://computer.howstuffworks.com/myspace.htm.

Troubled Times Ahead?

In 2005, MySpace was acquired by News Corp, a company run by conservative media mogul Rupert Murdoch. This triggered the panic button for many indie music proponents. It also brought back memories of the heyday of MP3.com, the indie music oasis that everyone was raving about just a few short years ago. Of course, that site eventually struggled, was bought out, and promptly dismantled.

Even with the Rupert Murdoch buyout, Anderson and DeWolfe still run MySpace and say they will continue to have free rein to operate it as they see fit. Let's hope that's the case, but time will tell.

Another problem is the increasing number of news reports about sexual predators using the site to gain access to the teens who frequent it. MySpace has appointed a new Chief Security Officer to step up efforts to improve safety while attempting to preserve the site's identity as a mecca for freewheeling self-expression.

Why I Wrote This Book

For months I researched MySpace to uncover how the most successful acts use it to reach thousands of fans, make connections, and advance their music careers. What I discovered along the way is that most artists misuse the many free features that MySpace offers and simply don't squeeze the most potential out of them.

I searched far and wide for useful how-to information on MySpace music marketing ... and couldn't find any. So I decided to publish something myself to help my many indie music readers, subscribers and customers. The result of that effort is this book.

Now let's move on to the stuff you really want to know ...

How to Set Up a Killer MySpace Profile

The Basics: Signing up

If you don't have a MySpace music page yet, go to www.myspace.com. Then click the Music section link, then look for the Artist Signup link.

Warning: You don't want to register with a general account because it won't give you all the goodies of an Artist account. So make sure you're signing up as an Artist.

> *"Bands are going to MySpace because it's free and they don't have to know how to do a web site ... [and] because there are millions of people on MySpace."*
>
> —Tom Anderson

Fine-Tuning Your MySpace Home Page for Maximum Punch

I won't walk you through every detail, because it's all spelled out for you on the site, but here are some essential notes on what to do with your profile page:

IMPORTANT: Even if you've been on MySpace for a while and think you know all these basic details, I encourage you to look over the following tips anyway. Make sure you are making the most of every MySpace feature.

Editing Your Profile

Click the Edit Profile link and you have four options:

1. Upcoming Shows

This is obviously where you post all of your upcoming gigs. Be sure to supply complete details — everything a fan would need to know to attend.

2. Band Details

This is a crucial section that deserves extra attention in the following areas:

> **Headline** — This little section is often poorly used by many artists. Use it to clearly describe your style of music. If you have a

descriptive motto, such as "electronica for lovers," put it in this Headline section. Don't waste this prime real estate!

Bio — Here's where you put a brief story of who you are, what you play, and why people should care. Remember, you can use HTML in these sections, so I recommend you include live links to specific pages on your main (non-MySpace) web site. Invite people to check out your additional song samples, sign up on your mailing list, view pictures from your latest tour — and include direct links to these pages within this Bio text.

Members — Include interesting info on the members of your band or, if you're a solo act, the members of your support team (co-writer, producer, manager, etc).

"Have short (or at least clear and easy to read) information. Not many people are going to sit through a whole page of something like a band bio if it's too long or hard to read."
-Elizabeth Mauban

Influences and Sounds Like — These two sections are also essential to targeting the right fans on MySpace. Complete this statement: "I would love to connect with people who are fans of ..." List as many well-known acts as are appropriate. Then list those names in these two boxes. These sections do come up in search results, so make them count!

Website — Obviously, put the link to your main artist home page — preferably YourName.com. You do have one, right? As you'll see in the artist survey coming up, the most successful acts do NOT use MySpace as their primary web site.

Record Label and Label Type — This is simply where you list the name of your label (whether you're signed to one or started one yourself) and the type of label. If you're unsigned, be sure to proudly display "indie."

Extra note on the Headline section (mentioned on the previous page): Some successful acts use this area to announce their latest CD releases. Here are some examples:

- Nickelback proclaimed "FAR AWAY — THE NEW SINGLE — IN STORES NOW!"

- The Veronicas similarly typed in "The Secret Life of ... In Stores Now!"

- And Shiny Toy Guns announced "album now available — www.shinytoyguns.com." (Nice touch putting their web site here.)

3. Basic Info

What you type in the Band Name section will show prominently at the top of your home page. You can put the name of your band, your solo artist name, the name of your company, whatever is most fitting. Also fill in the sections for city, state, country and zip code.

4. Manage Songs

This is where you upload and edit the settings for the four songs you can place in the music player on your page. Here you can allow visitors to add songs to their profile pages, auto-play the first song when someone views your profile, or randomize the song play. When you upload, you can also control whether people can download or only stream each track. I suggest giving some away and holding some back. But that's up to you.

Two hot tips on song files:

- Here's something hardly anyone does ... Create a special file that is a sampling of several songs. A verse and chorus, then fade out and into another song, etc. Maybe include excerpts from five of your best songs. Give this file away free. Include a spoken word bit at the end where you thank people for listening and invite them to visit your site to purchase the entire CD.

- Before you upload your MP3s, make sure you have filled out the ID tags within the file. Include the song title, artist name, album title. I also suggest you include your web site address behind your artist name. (To edit these tags, right-click the file name while it plays in a program such as MusicMatch Jukebox or Windows Media Player. Look for an Edit ID Tags option in the menu.)

One more important song file note: MySpace users can rate (and therefore rank) any song listed in an artist's MySpace music player. Encourage your fans to do so. The music player on your profile page also displays how many times each song has been played. The best rated and most listened to songs appear the highest on the MySpace music charts.

"Actively solicit your MySpace friends for help in getting gigs and support." -Scott Andrew

So, from the beginning, choose four songs that you will want to keep there for a long time. Because when you upload a fresh song, the count goes back to zero.

5. Listing Info

This is where you set your MySpace URL, as in www.myspace.com/yourname and your genre categories. Be accurate with the genre selections so the right people can find you!

Selecting and Uploading Your Photos

Click the **Upload / Change Photos** link. There you can select up to 12 photos to include in your photo section, which people can view when they click the **View more pics** link on your profile page. Be sure to select your best, most-striking photo as your "default" picture, which is the one that displays on your profile page and along with all the comments you leave on others' pages.

Important: Spend a few bucks (or twist the arm of a photographer pal) and get good photos.

As indie musician John Pippus says, "I can't stress enough the importance of getting professional quality band pics. I paid a friend of a friend $100 and he shot a roll in his studio, and it makes such a difference to the image I want to portray. Cheesy digital photos, shot with a flash, just scream amateur!"

Note that MySpace users can also rate each other's photos.

Tweaking Your Account and Profile Settings

In the **Account Settings** section is a list of options to look over. One is the e-mail address at which you receive MySpace notifications. Make sure it's an address you check regularly.

Another one to note is **Profile Settings**. There you can determine whether people can post HTML messages. Allowing HTML can lead to a lot of big, slow-loading files on your profile page. So you might consider clicking the boxes here to keep things lean and mean.

Considering More MySpace Settings

The **Edit Comments** section allows you to delete unwanted entries others have left in your Comments box. Also check out the Manage Calendar and Manage Address Book links for more options.

"Don't spend too much time on MySpace and forget to practice!"
–Chris Holmes

Spicing Up Your Page's Look & Feel — Without Getting Nauseous

MySpace allows users to customize the entire look of their profile page — including the layout, fonts and colors. Unfortunately, too many artists take advantage of this feature with horrific results.

My best advice: Keep your page layout lean and clean. Clashing colors, annoying background images, and hard-to-read typefaces will not endear you to fans. Spicing it up is one thing; making people seasick is another.

Effective tactics: Get creative and think of ways you can make your profile more enticing — and more likely to "capture" MySpace surfers who are potential fans. Here are two ideas you might consider:

- The band Hawthorne Heights included a clickable image with the text "Discover the Secret of 'If Only You Were Lonely.'" The link led to a PDF file that explained the messages hidden within the clever CD sleeve design of its latest release. Any time you can tease people with a "secret," they're more likely to learn more.

- Many smart artists embed a mailing list signup form right into their MySpace profile. But don't just ask for an e-mail address. Offer to give fans special access to your subscriber-only music goodies package ... if only they fill out the form and hit Submit.

For more page design tips, MySpace has a forum dedicated to customizing profiles at http://forum.myspace.com/.

Note: You'll have to log in to access this forum. Derek Punsalan posted a popular Squidoo lens on **How to Create a Custom MySpace Overlay** at www.squidoo.com/myspace_div_overlay/.

Other MySpace layout tools can be found at MySpace Toolbox (www.myspacetoolbox.com) and MySpace Support (www.myspacesupport.com).

Promoting Your Web Address

Countless artists are now hyping their MySpace web page to fans. And that's great. You want your people to know you have a presence on the ever-popular mega-site. But remember what happened to MP3.com? Thousands of bands did the same thing during that site's heyday. Once it went under, every MP3.com artist web address was suddenly lost.

Don't make that mistake here. I'm sure MySpace won't go anywhere soon. But we live in an era of unprecedented change. Stuff happens. So be prepared.

Your best bet: Register your own artist domain name. If you have a regular web site apart from MySpace (and you should), list both addresses, as in:

www.MyBand.com
www.myspace.com/myband

That way, if one goes down, all your promo material has an alternate address where fans can find you. And if both sites stay around forever, you have provided two great ways to hunt you down.

If MySpace is your only web presence, cough up the 9 bucks a year to register a domain name, and simply have it redirect to your MySpace page. If the big site ever flounders, you can just point your domain somewhere else — and never lose touch with your fans.

"Now that MySpace is here, you don't need a label to be heard ... The world is all about energy. If you can generate energy, it will ultimately translate into money."
–Billy Corgan

Using MySpace to Turbo-Charge Your Indie Music Career

It should go without saying, but to make the most of this social networking site you must be willing to "network" and be "social." You won't benefit much from MySpace by simply setting up a page and letting it run itself.

One of the first things you should do once you're set up is to start **Making Friends**!

This is where the networking part comes into play. For anything to happen, you must make "friends" with other people on MySpace. There are many types of people and companies that you should target to be your friend.

Here are the seven most important for your music career:

- **Fans** — people who will enjoy your music and rave about you to their friends

- **Other artists** — people with whom you can network, share gigs and resources, and cross-promote

- **Venues** — people who work for the places where you'd like to perform

- **Radio stations and shows** — people who host or produce shows on which you'd like airplay

- **Music publications** — people who run the e-zines, newspapers, magazines, etc., in which you'd like to get exposure

- **Independent filmmakers** — people who may want to use your music in their movies

- **Music events, companies and organizations** — people who operate businesses and associations that support indie music

There are two basic ways to build a list of friends: outgoing and incoming requests. Let's examine each one ...

"Send messages to all of the bands in your area. Eventually, they will need someone to play a show with, and you'll be first on their list."
-Mia Kaminsky

Making Friend Requests — Outgoing

When seeking people to be your friend, you want to be effective. After all, there are tens of millions of registered users on the site. You don't have the time to wade through thousands of profiles that aren't in line with your musical style or career direction.

Luckily, there are many ways to hunt down your ideal friends and fans on MySpace:

- **Use the Search feature** — Click the general Search link and you'll be taken to ... you guessed it, the Search page. At the top you can search all of MySpace or just certain areas of the site (such as Music, Blogs, Books) using certain keywords. For grins, I put in "Elvis Costello" and came up with 5,000 results. You can enter the names of bands that sound like yours and find out exactly who their fans are on MySpace.

  You can also use the "Affiliations for Networking" search tool (a little farther down the page). With this you search by topics and areas of interest. This would be especially good for tracking down industry people and companies.

- **Look through the Friends list of similar artists** — Go to any artist's page, scroll down to their Friend Space section, and click

"View All of [Artist's Name] Friends." If you think fans of that artist might enjoy your music, you'll find a gold mine of perfect potential fans waiting for you in their Friends list.

- **Look through the Comments section of similar artists** — Also on every artist's page is a Friends Comments section at the bottom. People who post here are not only friends and fans of the artist, but they are the most active MySpacers. The most recent comment is always at the top of the list, which lets you know which fans have just been on this artist's page.

  Zero in on the people who leave meaningful comments. You might want to pass over those who just mindlessly shout "Dude, you rock!" Unless, of course, you're wanting to cater to the "Dude, you rock!" crowd.

- **Use the Browse feature** — This one may not be the most effective, but in the Browse section you can search for people based on zip code, age, gender, and a number of other criteria. This was probably originally set up for people interested in online dating, but it could be useful for music marketing too.

Once you visit someone's profile page and determine that he or she is a good potential friend ...

- **Click the "Add to Friends" link** (usually located under their main photo on the left).

- **Confirm** that you really want to add the person.

Most people will just move on to the next "Add to Friends" prospect. Then they sit back and wait to be accepted and added to the person's network. But many successful artists suggest you also leave the person a message to begin forming a relationship. To do so, just click the "Send Message" link (right above the "Add to Friends" link). A good idea if you can make time to do it.

"It shouldn't be about how big your fan list looks. What's more impor-tant is that you can convert those fans into ticket buyers, CD sales and promoters. If you go around adding everybody, chances are they'll listen to you once and never again."

–Katie McGowan

Accepting Friend Requests — Incoming

Once you've spent a little time on MySpace, you'll find you not only can add friends by actively seeking them out ... they will start seeking you out and making friend requests of you.

This can be a good thing. All you have to do is log into your MySpace account and accept them. You can even bulk accept a group of friend requests all at one time.

NOTE: This is where artists' philosophies vary greatly. Some strive to rack up as many friends as possible. Indeed, many bands demonstrate their popularity with the sheer number of friends they have — sometimes tens or hundreds of thousands of people. But other artists prefer to limit the number of people they accept and concentrate on developing relationships with quality people who truly want to network and cross-promote. It's your call.

"It's all about relationships. People like to connect with others. Especially if you are sincere in what you do, people will be drawn to you simply by your authenticity and initiative."

-Branon Dempsey

Leaving and Receiving Comments

Once you are someone's "friend" (whether you accepted them or they accepted you), the next best thing to do is visit each new friend's profile page and post a comment. To do so, just scroll to the very bottom of their page and click the "Add Comment" link.

Comments are effective because, not only does the artist whose page you're on read what you write, but every person who visits that artist's page can see your comment as well.

There are two different ways to leave MySpace comments: the smart way and the dumb way.

- **The Dumb Way** — post a generic "thanks for the add" message or pre-produced image that says the same thing, along with a "check out my music" plea. If you're new to MySpace, "Add" in this case refers to the person's willingness to "Add" a friend. Everybody leaves this sort of bland, mindless message. So if you want to blend in with everyone else on MySpace, join in the parade.

- **The Smart Way** — post a quick message that is at least slightly meaningful and personalized about the person whose page you're visiting. Make a reference to their song or musical influences (if they are an artist) or favorite book or something (if they are just a fan). Instead of begging people to come listen to your music, end your comment with your name and a cool "sig file" that includes an intriguing motto and link to your main web site and MySpace page.

Example: Regarding that comment sig file ... a statement such as "Find out why *Music Buzz* magazine called the Purple Cows music 'punk rock for college geeks'" is much better than a lame "Let me know what you think of my tunes, man."

Tip: When one of your friends leaves a new comment on your page, return the favor by leaving a relevant comment on their page. This increases your exposure level on the site.

Suggestion: Regularly monitor the comments being left on your MySpace profile page. I suggest you delete the ones that are senseless or just filled with boneheaded hype (unless that's the type of fan you want to attract). Make sure your friend's comments reflect the type of vibe you want to put out.

Note: You can set up your profile so that any new comments aren't posted until you approve them. To do this, go to your Home admin area, click Account Settings, then Privacy Settings.

Leaving and Receiving Messages

MySpace has an internal e-mail messaging system (as well as an Instant Message feature) that allows you to send personal, non-public messages to any other MySpace user.

Here are some key tips on leaving and receiving messages:

- **Use the Send Message feature for private notes to people**. But ... if the content of your message is not too personal in nature, you'll get more exposure impact by posting the same message in the person's public Friends Comments section. That way, your message is more likely to be seen by others who may discover you.

- **Include your e-mail sig file and live links**. When sending someone a message, be sure to include your name, slogan and web site links. The MySpace message system also allows you to use HTML, so you can create live links and even include images. But do so sensibly.

- **Stay on top of your incoming messages**. Since you're using MySpace to network and get exposure, you must be responsive to people. So it's important to regularly check your incoming messages and respond — if a response is required. Also, consider the note earlier and think about responding to people's messages by posting your reply in their public Comments section.

Posting Bulletins

This is perhaps one of the most useful MySpace features. Use it to communicate with all of your MySpace friends at one time. The messages you send here aren't actually e-mailed to people in the usual sense, but they will appear in the MySpace Bulletin Inboxes of everyone on your friends list — whether that's 200 people or 200,000. A pretty nifty tool.

(For an awesome tip on a sneaky way to send e-mail bulletins to your fans, see the "Hotter Tip" item in the Blog section coming up.)

Use common sense with this feature. Don't bombard friends with useless announcements, but do use it to keep in touch with people when you have news of note. Some examples might be:

- You just posted a new free download
- You just won an award or got some type of media coverage
- You need you fans' help to win an online music poll
- You just released a new CD

Adding Upcoming Shows

I briefly mentioned the Upcoming Shows feature earlier when discussing the Edit Profile link. But it deserves extra attention here. Make sure to add all of your live performances, in-store appearances, conference showcases, and any other events that would be appropriate. Fill out all of the sections. Be thorough.

When people search MySpace for things to do in your area, your event listing will show up. That's free exposure just waiting to happen, so be sure to take advantage of it!

Selecting Your 'Top 8'

As I mentioned earlier, you can get access to any artist's army of friends by clicking the "View All of [Artist's Name] Friends" link on their profile page. But, as you probably already know, you can select eight friends to display prominently on your main page.

By default, MySpace displays the eight friends that have been MySpace users the longest. But there are some effective ways to use this little feature for greater impact. Here are two of them:

- Select prominent artists in your genre to reinforce the type of company you want to be associated with. As you know, most well-known acts these days have a MySpace presence. Seek out the artists whose fan bases best overlap with yours. Request to be added as one of their friends, and once accepted, add those acts to your Top 8.

- Use your Top 8 slots to cross-promote with other similar indie acts. This is from the "show mine and I'll show yours" school of thought, and a lot of acts claim to get promotional pop from it. It works best with acts you already know and perhaps have even performed with before.

Requesting Song Adds

MySpace allows any user to add a streaming version of any artist's song to their personal profile page. It doesn't take a genius to figure out how valuable this feature can be.

Here are two tips for making this work:

- Be sure to allow users to add your song. It's not a default setting with your player. You must manually activate it. To do so, go to your MySpace admin Home, then select Edit Profile, then Manage Songs, and click the appropriate check box.

- Ask your fans to add your song. Make it a contest. Every fan who adds your song is

entered into a drawing. Give away something small (a digital download perhaps) to
everyone who does it. Offer a big prize to
one lucky winner (maybe a spot in your Top
8 for a month).

Posting to Your Blog

To publish a post to your personal blog, first click
Manage Blog, then scroll down and look for the Post
New Blog link. (You'd think there'd be a quicker way
to take this step, but I can't find one.)

Regularly adding to your blog is yet another way to
communicate with your fans and give people a reason
to return to your profile. Another cool thing is that
blog posts are searchable, so if you fill them with
keywords related to your genre and music, fans may
more easily find you. Also, use your blog to have a
conversation with people. It's not just a place to hype
your CDs, gigs and merch, although you should
definitely feel free to tastefully plug what you have
available.

Here are just some of the kinds of topics you can post
to your MySpace blog:

- Stories of what happened at particular live
  shows
- The circumstances that influenced your
  lyrics

- Interesting things that happened to you while on tour
- Media exposure you've just received
- Awards or acclaim you've just earned
- Full lyrics to your original songs

Here are a few creative blog posts I found from MySpace artists:

- John of Secondhand Serenade asked his fans for their opinions on his upcoming T-shirt and sweatshirt designs.

- The Hollywood Undead (which was one of the first indie bands signed to the MySpace Records label) announced a street team contest on their blog. They asked fans to promote the band and then send photos of what they did. The most creative fan promoters won prizes and even made an appearance in the band's next video.

- Chantelle Paige posted answers to common questions about singing, acting and modeling.

As you can see, there are lots of great ways to use your MySpace blog.

Advice: Always write your blog posts in the first and second person, as in "I (or we) had a great time at the gig last night. Thank you for everything you do to support my (or our) music!" Avoid dry third-person wording, such as "The band will make an appearance on the Z-100 morning show tomorrow. They appreciate your support!" Be personal, not distant.

Hot Tip (if your CD is available on Amazon.com): Ask your friends to plug your CD in their own blog posts. MySpace has a feature that allows users to fill in a "What I'm reading/listening to" section at the end of blog posts. The chosen book or CD is turned into a link to the title's sales page on Amazon (no doubt with an affiliate link that MySpace earns some change on).

If your fans are posting to their blogs anyway, why not have them mention your CD while they're at it?

Hotter Tip: Encourage fans to subscribe to your blog. When they do, every time you post a new blog entry, they get an e-mail notification — something that doesn't happen with the more common Bulletin post.

Joining Groups

If you've ever belonged to a Yahoo Groups or Topica list, you know what the online groups concept is. It's yet another way to create a virtual community of like-minded people. Well, MySpace has its own Groups section, with more than 30 topic categories. As of this writing, the Music section alone has nearly 200,000 groups, and the number of Fan Club groups totals almost 117,000.

Here are some examples of MySpace groups and the number of members each has:

- Green Day — 137,409
- Hip-Hop Nation — 78,782
- Linkin Park — 73,622
- Napoleon Dynamite — 60,034
- Marilyn Manson Fans — 35,016
- Victoria's Secret — 35,998
- Dance Dance Revolution — 26,042

I purposely included some non-musical groups to point out the various ways you can target potential fans. Do the people most attracted to your music share a common interest in any of the following?

- A particular movie, TV show or book
- A certain religion or spiritual practice
- A geographic location or vacation destination
- A specific hobby, pastime or lifestyle
- A particular occupation or cause

Think outside the box and use MySpace groups to reach the people most likely to enjoy your music!

Important: All the rules from earlier sections apply — any communicating you do within the Groups section should be thoughtful, personalized, and avoid hype.

Creating Your Own Group

If you don't mind the extra effort, you could also start your own MySpace group. Of course, you could create your own fan club, or enlist a hardcore fan to run it. Or ... you could start a group around the topic of your specific genre — which, in my opinion, has the potential to lure more fans.

Here are some music group topic ideas:

- Classical Music for Brainiacs
- The Trip-Hop Resource Center
- Best Smooth Jazz Albums of All Time
- The Alt-Country Clearinghouse

By running a group on your overall genre, you will attract more fans in general. And, because you are the group moderator, you benefit (and get exposure) by being the expert who runs the whole thing!

Working the Forums

Similar to the Groups section is the Forums area. It's basically the MySpace version of an old-school message board (from back in the days when no one had ever heard of a blog or podcast). Click around the Forums section and see if there's a place for you to post a relevant message or make a mutually beneficial connection.

Uploading Your Videos

This is a newer section, and it looks to be a promising way to promote your music on MySpace — if you have a digital video available. Click the Video link and you'll be able to browse thousands of streaming videos already available on the site. Most importantly, you can upload your own videos — and then encourage your fans to add them to their profile pages.

Don't have a slick music video? No problem. Grab a digital video camera and shoot some footage of a rehearsal or live show or life on the road ... or shoot your own exclusive interview with the band. Whatever you do, get something along these lines up on MySpace.

Tip: If you use a PC runing Windows XP, check your Accessories folder for something called Windows Movie Maker. This great little free program allows you to edit together sound, video and still pictures. It even has a lot of cool effects and various ways you can save your finished files. If you don't have access to pro editing software, there's a lot you can do with Movie Maker.

"Don't make a mess of your site.
Keep it clean and effective."
-Michael Ahlström

Scouring the Music Directory

Would you like to hunt down complimentary artists and bands that might like to cross-promote with you? The Music Directory is the place to go. To get there, go to the main MySpace Music section, then click the **Directory** link.

There you can search artists by genre and name. Example: In the Power Pop genre, there are 48 pages of listings under the letter S alone. Sounds like a great place to find new indie music allies.

Using Music Search

While in the main Music section, click the **Search** link. There you can look up artists by genre, country, state, and zip code. You can also do narrow searches for keywords listed in the Band Bio, Influences or Sounds Like categories. And you can sort search results by the artists' number of plays, friends, or how long they've been on MySpace. Pretty cool.

Posting in Classifieds

Another nice MySpace feature is the free Classifieds section. This is probably the Craigslist.com-inspired section of the site. I'm not sure how effective it is for music promotion, but here are some categories that might be useful:

Under **MUSICIAN XCHANGE**
- positions and openings
- instruments for sale
- instruments wanted

Under **MYSPACE FRIENDS**
- artists
- musicians

Under **SERVICES**
- creative
- event
- lessons

Under **CASTING CALLS**
- musicians

Under **FOR SALE**
- cds / dvds / vhs
- musical instruments
- tickets

Note: The only time I used MySpace Classifieds to promote my books, the one response I got was from a guy who claimed he wanted to buy a bunch of my books and have them shipped to Nigeria.

Yes, beware of scammers!

Checking Out Chat Rooms and Schools

Go to the main MySpace home page (not your Home admin page) and you'll see links to Chat Rooms and Schools. In the **Chat Rooms** section, you can choose a specific topic category, geographic location, or age group … then enter a live chat room where you interact with others online using text. As always, targeting is key.

In the **Schools** section, you can search for a specific high school, college or university. The idea here is that past and present students join school lists. Each school list has a moderator, similar to MySpace Groups, and members can post messages and communicate with each other.

Obviously, if you currently attend or previously attended a particular school, you should look up that school and join its list. Then let fellow students know about your music.

Considering MySpace Adder Software, Bots and Whore Trains

I mentioned at the beginning of this book that when I searched for useful MySpace self-promotion tips and resources, I couldn't find any. However, one thing there seems to be an abundance of is automated software that will add MySpace friend requests, comments, and more for you — literally while you sleep.

Why are these short-cut resources so plentiful? Because working MySpace properly can take a lot of time and energy. It's a sad statement that so many quick-fix solutions sprang up long before any practical hands-on marketing resources existed.

I'm not going to discuss these automated programs here, but if you are interested in learning more about them, search Google for "MySpace adder" or "MySpace bot."

Warning: I've never used these automated adders. And I caution you to think twice before investing in and using them yourself. Word has it that MySpace does not condone these programs and may delete profiles that use such software. So proceed at your own risk.

Whoretrains are simply electronic versions of a chain letter or pyramid scheme, whereby you add your name to a list, then every person on the list adds each other to their Myspace Friends list.

"You have to keep up on your site by logging in to connect with other users, check mail, etc. Like anything else in marketing, if you leave your site on the shelf and don't work the buzz, people will pass by."
   —Branon Dempsey

Top Tips from the MySpace Survey

Prior to publishing this book, I asked readers of my e-zine and blog to send me their best MySpace marketing tips. I also sought out advice from select industry people. Man, did I get an avalanche of great responses.

The bulk of the rest of this book is made up of the full-length responses I received from 30 artists, managers and promoters who use MySpace to market themselves or the artists they work with. I suggest you take the time to read all of their tips.

However, to help you digest the key tactics they reveal, I've highlighted what I consider to be their best tips over the next several pages. Look over these excerpts, then read each person's complete response in the next section.

- Make sure you post regular bulletins to your growing fan base. Don't just have them sign up and then ignore them. The whole point

of MySpace is to build the communication network. Anytime there's a show or a new song or whatever, post it to the list.
-Mark Hansen

- Send messages to all of the bands in your area, acquainting yourself with them. Eventually, they will need someone to play a show with, and you'll be on their list of first contacts. **-Mia Kaminsky**

- Actively solicit your MySpace friends for help in getting gigs and support. A great example: my friends in Everyday Jones (www.myspace.com/everydayjones) do a great job of using their MySpace page to urge fans to action. **-Scott Andrew**

- The first thing I did was to search for females age 18 to 35 within a 250-mile radius of my location. This involved looking at profiles from every result that was returned, determining their musical tastes and, if their tastes were in line with our music, sending both a friend request *and* an e-mail explaining who we are, what we do, and why I think they would like us.
-Steve Senes

- MySpace allows bands to upload four songs. With our music being as diverse as it is, four songs is not enough. So what I've done is place a banner towards the top of the page which, when clicked, will open a new window (or tab) containing a Flash-based music player loaded with all 14 tracks from our demo. The MP3 files and player are hosted on the server for our web site. This way, people can, at their leisure, check out the entire CD and get an accurate picture of the band. I've had a lot of people comment favorably on this feature. -**Steve Senes**

- I search for bands in a state by the amount of fans they have. Say I want to do Iowa. I will search rock bands in Iowa, by the amount of fans they have. Then I will go to their comments and add as many of the people who have left them comments as possible. This helps because I know that if the fans are leaving comments, they will usually actually take a listen to the music. -**Dave Bovyn**

- You have to keep up on your site by logging in to connect with other users, check mail, etc. Like anything else in marketing, if you leave your site on the shelf and not work the buzz, people will pass by. It's all about relationships — people like to connect with others, especially if you are sincere in what you do, people will be drawn to you simply by your authenticity and initiative. -**Branon Dempsey**

- Whenever possible, try to follow up your friend request with a message that connects with them, like "*Zoolander* is my favorite movie, too!" or "Where did you get that cool background?" -**Darrel Kathan**

- We use our profile as an EPK (electronic press kit) of sorts. It contains our streaming music, our bio, schedule, pictures, our blog, e-mail sign up, who we sound like/influences and *feedback from fans*. This allows fans to see what other people think about us and gives club owners a chance to see if our crowd is the right fit — or if we can even pull a crowd. -**Chris Holmes**

- Don't make a mess of your site. All these streaming features and extra graphics that are linked in will take an eon to load and people may miss what you're trying to accomplish. Keep it clean and effective. -**Michael Ahlström**

- Stick with it. Their are a lot of new people signing up every day who go there to network. Maybe not everyone wants to network with *you* but everyone wants to feel good and have a good time and that's what you sell them, if they let you. -**Darrel Kathan**

- Create separate profiles for each of your band members. Remember, those people you went to high school with? They might search for you and not make fun of you for being in a band. My personal profile has been invaluable for showing those people that I *can* make a living playing music while they work some lame 9-5. -**Chris Holmes**

- Don't spend too much time on MySpace and forget to practice! -**Chris Holmes**

- Encourage your new friends on MySpace to use one of your songs as the default song on their page. You'll get more traffic if their friends like the song. -**Catherine Duc**

- In the "about me" section, I've put "hot" links to other MySpace artists who I've done session work for. Often in return, they will put a "hot" link back to my page. It works! -**Craig Ferguson**

- When I send out bulletins for shows or newsletters, I always put at the end of my message, "If you know of any venues, festivals, parties or bands that you think would fit the Blue Island Tribe, let us know." This has become a great success for booking in markets that I have not even thought about breaking into. -**James Frey**

- It's not the quantity of friends you have, it's the quality of friends. I have seen plenty of bands that have 2,000 friends, but have only 250 plays. That means that yes, they are making "friends," but no one is really taking the time to listen. It's better to have a smaller number of friends that you truly connect with and talk to. -**Nick Mitchell**

- Make sure and stop by your friends' spaces and leave comments every so often so they don't forget about you. Again, fight the urge to post a form message. Make it personal. This will keep the friendships alive. This is especially important for fans.
  -**Nick Mitchell**

- Targeted messaging. First of all, I search MySpace profiles to find people who like our kind of music. Fans of artists who have influenced our sound will likely enjoy our music as well. Then I send an introductory message introducing our group and inviting them to visit our profile page. Approximately one in three people have responded by sending friend requests and/or giving us positive feedback. -**Andrew Gilpin**

- Many clothing and print companies on MySpace are interested in working with bands who have a strong fan base. Cross-promotion can be really effective, even online! -**Katie McGowan**

- Competitions. Everybody loves a competition and it's so simple to get fans involved on MySpace. Competitions for merch, free tickets, even a place in the MySpace "Top 8" have gone down very well for Submerse and have been used to spread the word of the band. -**Katie McGowan**

- It shouldn't be about how big your fan list looks. What's more important is that you can convert those fans into ticket buyers, CD sales and promoters. If you go around adding everybody, chances are they'll listen to you once and never again.
  -**Katie McGowan**

- Have a slam-dunk profile picture. Sad to say, but most people see before they hear. To attract more potential fans to your site, you have to get them interested based on visual alone. But we mean *classy* visual. For musicians, that's either a dynamite shot that isn't like every other typical band shot, or even a really creative logo or visually stunning picture that can wrap around what your music is all about. After you get them to come and look a little deeper, you reel 'em in with your amazing and undeniable music. The point is to drive traffic to your site, and then let the art speak for you.
  -**Kate and Kacey Coppola**

- Join groups that either reflect the type of music you make, have members that match your target fan profile, or just interest you in general. This is a much better way to make yourself known to potential fans than by randomly asking every new profile you come across to add your band. That is like catching a fly with chopsticks — a nice idea, but very hard to do.
  -Kate and Kacey Coppola

- Never use "whore trains" or any such thing. Yes, some people add off of those, but they most likely just want their number of friends to go up. You want real fans who care about you, so a number hunter isn't going to cut it. **-Elizabeth Mauban**

- Have short (or at least clear and easy to read) information. Not many people are going to sit through a whole page of something like a band bio if it's too long or hard to read. **-Elizabeth Mauban**

- MySpace is only one channel. The important thing is to give to people — only *then* will something come back to you, and not always from where you expect it. Sending Friend requests, posting comments, answering messages, showing your presence (on MySpace and elsewhere) will result in web site visitors and more. **-Andrea Gera**

- Share experiences, sorrows and happy moments. Connect. This will create traffic and draw attention to you — if you have something worthy to say or sing, that is. **-Menios Symeon**

- Do not ever say "thanks for the add." That is the most overused cliché on MySpace. **-John Pippus**

- If a picture is worth a thousand words than load up on pictures. Glue Gun has a song entitled "Eva's Got a Mohawk," so our default photo is a chick with a mohawk. It's like a magnet for punk rockers, which is exactly what our fan base is. **-Bob Oedy**

- Forget about the "Friends Counter." It's not about having 10,000+ friends. It's about having 100 true fans who are waiting for you to drop that record. I typically narrow my friend searches based on interests and keywords. **-Renee Sebastian**

- I've compared my music to that of other known artists and was very specific. One person bought a CD just based on the description because she likes all of the artists mentioned. **-Jennifer Richman**

Survey of 30 Indie Music People

Here are the raw, full-length responses from the 30 artists, managers and promoters who responded to my MySpace Music Marketing Tips survey. Note the range of experiences and techniques used. Some artist's tactics contradict those used by others. Regardless, I know you're smart enough to take in all of their views and decide for yourself which ideas will work best for you.

Jeff Risden
Manager of **Relient K** and **House of Heroes**
www.myspace.com/relientk
www.myspace.com/houseofheroes

General thoughts on MySpace as a promotion tool:

MySpace is a great promotional tool for several reasons. For one, it's easy to use — from creating the personal web URL for the band to how easy it is to upload songs and set up your music, tour dates, and other info. The community aspect is a huge asset in setting up a virtual street team among fans through the site. The ability for bands to get on the site and communicate directly with their fans in a personal manner is also big.

Relient K has seen many new fans come to the band through their MySpace site. By introducing the band's music to people who wouldn't have otherwise heard the songs, we've seen album sales increase, concert attendance increase, and a greater awareness of the band in general among the public.

Top MySpace marketing tips:

- Have fans put you in their Top 8 so their friends can check out the band.

- Post bulletins about upcoming shows, events, news, etc.

- Blog, blog, blog! Kids/fans want to know what's going on with their favorite bands, and potential fans want to know more about who you are.

- Run contests via your MySpace site for tickets, merchandise, CDs, and calls from the band.

- Use the event function to let people know of your upcoming shows in their area.

Biggest MySpace drawbacks:

Many bands tend to over promote themselves through MySpace. There are some bands I'll get a ridiculous number of bulletins from and it just turns me off. Be strategic about the messages you send. If I get too many from a band, I start to ignore all of their bulletins, and that defeats the purpose the band has for sending them.

There are also over two million artist profiles on MySpace. That's a lot of competition to battle to find new fans and an audience — especially when most of those artists are going after the same people your band is.

Additional MySpace thoughts:

MySpace is like the ultimate EPK (electronic press kit). Everything is there — music, bio, tour dates, video, photos. Bands need to take their site seriously. Keep things clean and simple. A lot of bands fill up their site with skins that make loading and scrolling difficult and slow. They also have competing video/audio running at the same time which makes it difficult to figure out what you're supposed to be listening to.

The key for Relient K and my other band, House of Heroes, is just the ability to connect directly with their respective fans/potential fans. Kids desire this and for a band like RK, which isn't able to hang out for hours after shows meeting kids anymore due to the amount of kids coming to shows, it provides them the ability to still interact with their fans.

For House of Heroes, it allows them to meet new fans and get them personally engaged from the beginning. We also give away a lot of HOH comp tickets through their MySpace site for each show. It's a great way to get kids to come to their shows who wouldn't have come otherwise. And those kids, more often than not, come away from those shows as fans who have bought some merch too — which goes directly into the band's pockets.

Scott Andrew

www.myspace.com/scottandrewrawks

General thoughts on MySpace as a promotion tool:

I used to think it was THE way to find new fans online; now I think it's become just another tool to drive occasional traffic to my own site. There's just too much noise and chatter to make a deep impression. On the other hand, MySpace is still a must-do, given its popularity.

Top MySpace marketing tips:

- Target your ideal fans. Search for MySpacers who like music that resembles yours. For example, many of my GarageBand reviewers told me that some of my songs remind them of Guster. So I went to MySpace and did a search for Guster fans. Then I sent a short, very nicely worded invitation to be "friends."

- Mention in the invitation *why* you'd like to be friends (i.e. "Hey, you like Guster? People tell me I sound like Guster and I'm right here in town. Maybe we should be friends!"). This usually makes a better impression on the recipient, showing you've done a bit of research, setting you apart from the spammers.

- Make sure your MySpace page has big, obvious links to where people can buy your merch and sign up for your mailing list! Don't assume visitors will find your CD Baby page themselves. And actively solicit your MySpace friends for help in getting gigs and support. A great example: my friends in Everyday Jones (www.myspace.com/every dayjones) do a great job of using their MySpace page to urge fans to action.

Biggest MySpace drawbacks:

Super time-intensive. Search tools are slow and aren't very good. They used to offer "search within zip code" but they removed it.

Additional MySpace thoughts:

Please, *please* don't use MySpace as your sole web site!

Mark Hansen
Mark Hansen Music
www.myspace.com/mrkh

General thoughts on MySpace as a promotion tool:

I've been able to find my target audience much better than any other web-based effort. I make religious (Mormon) rock music, and my target is Mormon teenagers and twenty-somethings. There's a vast subculture of Mormon youth on MySpace, with thousands of users and hundreds of forum groups.

Top MySpace marketing tips:

- After making a friend request, go back to their profile and also send them a message. Tell them where you found them and specifically invite them to come check out your tunes. Not only is that more personal, but then they feel safer. There's no "Who is this and how did he find me?"

- When someone contacts you with a friend request, go to their profile and post a

"Thanks for the add" comment. That'll get your picture and profile at the top of their comment list for a while.

- Be active in the forums and groups that your audience frequents. Post comments often, and mention your music as often as is appropriate. Make your main picture a musical one (playing the guitar or some such) so that people make a connection and want to click to hear your tunes.

- Make sure you post regular bulletins to your growing fan base. Don't just have them sign up and then ignore them. The whole point of MySpace is to build the communication network. Anytime there's a show or a new song or whatever, post it to the list.

Biggest MySpace drawbacks:

Since my music is religiously based, I need to be careful of my friends list. I don't want to be exclusive, but I don't want it littered with the almost nude girls wanting people to come to their web-cam sites.

MySpace is getting a bad reputation and a lot of media coverage as an unsafe place full of predators. I need to be careful not to be viewed as a part of that, but still use the site effectively for promotion.

Mia Kaminsky
The Poor
www.myspace.com/givetothepoor

General thoughts on MySpace as a promotion tool:

It really connects me to fans and venues alike. I think it's great, although probably not the best way to do it.

Top MySpace marketing tips:

- Add friends like crazy. Go search for people within your zip code who have recently updated and add several pages worth. Some won't respond, but most will accept your add.

- Post a bulletin to all of your friends, even the out-of-towners, when you have a show booked. Give them reminders a week ahead of time, and then the day of (or the day before) the show.

- Send messages to all of the bands in your area, acquainting yourself with them. Eventually, they will need someone to play a show with, and you'll be on their list of first contacts.

Biggest MySpace drawbacks:

Sometimes people just don't check their MySpace enough or don't place much importance on it. It's frustrating when you get a response two or three weeks after you sent a message. Also, there are so many bands on MySpace that fans have lots to choose from. So, they may opt to see another band playing on the same night that they wouldn't have known about if it weren't for MySpace.

Additional MySpace thoughts:

LinkTiles.com is a great new site that connects all of your web pages — PureVolume, MySpace, etc, so fans never have to search for you.

Steve Senes
Nine Years Under
www.myspace.com/9yu

General thoughts on MySpace as a promotion tool:

I've found MySpace to be a killer way to network with potential fans as well as other bands (for future gigs) and other music business professionals. You can *never* have too many people listening to your stuff. Nine Years Under is a *very* new band, not yet playing live shows, yet through our MySpace persistence and our web presence, we've attracted the attention of a lot of people, including a successful Grammy-nominated producer who is now working with us to help us get to the next level. In our first two weeks on MySpace, we surpassed the 1,000 friends mark. Again, this is a band that hasn't yet played live. All of our promotion has been done using MySpace.

Top MySpace marketing tips:

The first thing I did was to search for females aged 18 to 35 within a 250-mile radius of my location. Seemed like a good place to start. This involved looking at profiles from every result that was returned, determining their musical tastes and, if their tastes were in line with the music we write, sending both a friend request and an e-mail explaining who we are, what we do, and why I think they would like us.

It's very time consuming to do it this way but, in my thinking, I hate spam and figure most people do also and would be irritated by someone whose musical style they can't stand hitting them up. Some people just want to inflate their friends list and will add you anyhow without checking you out, which isn't very helpful. Although people *do* check out others' friend lists and check out bands that way, so I suppose it is helpful.

I've also done a few so-called Whore Trains. I don't like these too much because, even though they've yielded some interested people, they've filled my bulletin space with crap like "Add this freak, she'll suck your Dad through a rubber hose" or other such garbage, as well as people who have no interest in you or your music.

There is one whoring technique that's really gotten me some good results though — www.freeflashtoys.com /thetrain.html. This is the Super Train and the results I've attained from using this have been mostly good. I get a lot of feedback on my music from people I've added using this tool. There seems to be a lot of people who are interested in new music on this thing.

Tip: Read the page and definitely do the "20 windows" thing. It definitely makes it quicker. Another tip: Internet Explorer users, keep one finger on your mouse, the other on Alt-F4. For Firefox, if you're set up to open new windows in tabs, the key shortcut to close tabs is Ctrl-W. Doing this can get you through the tabs/windows very quickly.

When you get friend requests from others, it pays to check out their profiles and make sure this is some-one who will likely dig your music. If not, you're likely to get a bunch of crap on your Comments section which, even if you have approval turned on, could be time consuming, to say the least.

I usually end up approving most requests though. Before I approve, I open their profile in a new window, go back to the approve window and approve, then post them a comment. If they don't have HTML turned off in their comments, I have a graphic I add with the band's logo and a short message thanking them for checking us out.

On our profile page, we have downloads turned off on the songs. When we were approaching 1,000 friend adds (in under two weeks), we sent out a bulletin and mails to some people on our list who had requested being able to download the songs. We said if we could reach 1,000 by a certain date, we'd open the downloads for three days. It worked. We went from 637 Tuesday night to 1,010 on Thursday afternoon. So I opened them for a few days.

Next thing I know, I'm having people add request me, saying they heard some of my music in a club and wanted to be added. Apparently, a few enterprising people burned the music to disc and took it to clubs where they had DJ friends play the stuff. Another person burned 100 CDs (he really likes the stuff) and asked if he could pass them out next time he goes out. Hey, since I was planning on giving away a "teaser" CD with four songs anyhow, I figured, Why not? This gets the music to people I probably couldn't and has netted me more fans.

Since we hit 1,000, I've not done a thing towards promotion, yet the list continues to grow. We're close to 1,400 now (tomorrow will be three weeks since we started on MySpace). Once the band actually starts playing, I look for this list to grow exponentially.

I can't stress enough, though, it's all about having

great songs. Without those, you really can't do much. This is also helping me spread the word. MySpace allows bands to upload four songs, which for a free site I guess is pretty generous. With our music being as diverse as it is, though, four songs cannot be an accurate representation, so what I've done is place a flashy banner towards the top of the page which, when clicked, will open a new window (or tab) containing a Flash-based music player loaded with all 14 tracks from our demo.

The MP3 files and player are hosted on the server for our web site. This way, people can, at their leisure, check out the entire CD and get an accurate picture of the band. I've had a lot of people comment favorably on this feature.

One more tip: It pays to customize your profile to match your band. Brand recognition, ya know? Just be cognizant of the person viewing your profile. If you load it up with all these flashing images, videos, blah, blah, blah ... it will bog down the computer when viewing the page and irritate the hell out of your potential fans. Not to mention those poor souls still tied to a dial-up connection.

I've actually left profiles without listening to the music because, by the time everything loads (MySpace is notoriously slow due to it's HUGE network of users), I'm bored of it all and move on. Others do too.

Also, since MySpace is so slow, it pays to have images

that you use in your profile, and in comments you leave for others, on your own server, such as those used for your web site. Trust me, it speeds things up a lot and makes the experience less painful for the end user.

Biggest MySpace drawbacks:

Other than being extremely time-consuming and having to deal with the occasional prepubescent asshole or wannabe ghetto thug, not really many drawbacks. Since the site is so slow, browsing through and viewing profiles to determine their tastes can take forever! But if you gain fans, it's well worth it.

Additional MySpace thoughts:

I think MySpace has gotten to be an invaluable tool to grow awareness of your band. If your music is good and appeals to people, they will wanna get on board and help you spread the word to people they know.

Dave Bovyn
Myllhouse
www.myspace.com/myllhouse

General thoughts on MySpace as a promotion tool:

We've had our MySpace page since the end of 2004. We would add our friends from around our town, but other then that, I wouldn't add anyone. We had 1,500 friends over the course of two years. But in the last two weeks, we have jumped from 1,500 to almost 4,000.

The main reason is because we have been booking some out-of-state shows for the summer. We haven't posted the dates yet, but I went ahead and started adding people from the states we'll be heading too, and it has gotten us a ton of fans. Here are my tricks.

- I search for bands in a state by the amount of fans they have. Say I want to do Iowa. I will search rock bands in Iowa, by the amount of fans they have. Then I will go to their comments and add as many of the people who have left them comments as possible. This helps because I know that if the fans are leaving comments, they will usually actually take a listen to the music, rather then blindly adding people because of what state they are from.

- I also search for people within five miles of the zip code of the venue we are playing and add them. Even if they don't specifically say they like our style of music, a lot of times people will come out because it is close to home, and then they end up diggin' the band.

- Banners are huge. We have a couple

different banners that people put up on their MySpace, and when surfers click on the banner, it sends them directly to our MySpace account.

- Bulletins also work wonders because they can be read by everyone on your friends list. So if you are promoting a show and you bulletin it, everyone who's on your friends list knows about it.

- It's also a huge deal to people if you leave them a comment. I know it's hard to leave everybody on your list a comment, but if they leave you one, it's great to leave them one back, because then all their friends see that you left them a comment, and maybe they will click your link from there!

Branon Dempsey
www.myspace.com/branondempsey

General thoughts on MySpace as a promotion tool:

I've been active on MySpace.com for the past three months and have gained quite a response. It's an invaluable tool because it's free, universal, user-friendly and people already know MySpace — as opposed to joe-bob.com.

Top MySpace marketing tips:

- When you sign up on MySpace, you can upload a picture next to your name and a message. That display is posted to any message, e-mail, comment or friend request that you initiate — on other people's MySpace pages. They easily can put your face and music to a name.

- Make friends — simply go to other people's spaces that are of interest and "add friend." A request will be sent to that owner and they will either accept or deny your request. In turn, other friends they have in their "friend list" will see you as a resident and may contact you to be a friend. People abroad on the MySpace web site like to identify with other users who have common interests — especially music.

- Once you become a friend, leave people comments to dialogue with them. In doing so, you can market your web site and music with a friendly message to "come and see." Again, other users will see your comment, message and picture, and it has more potential to create a buzz.

  From there you can further your dialoging with other users with an instant message or blog post. MySpace also tracks the number

of visitors and how many downloaded or
played your music — all for nothing!

I was pleasantly surprised at the response. When I
became active on the site, within two months I
already gained 400 people who not only visited my
site but checked out my music. Not bad once you get
going! Plus, I met really nice people along the way,
including old friends and connections.

Biggest MySpace drawbacks:

You have to keep up on your site by logging in to
connect with other users, check mail, etc. Like anything else in marketing, if you leave your site on the
shelf and not work the buzz, people will pass by. It's
all about relationships — people like to connect with
others, especially if you are sincere in what you do,
people will be drawn to you simply by your
authenticity and initiative.

Additional MySpace thoughts:

The site may be hard to order a pizza. Other than
that, MySpace is a great site! You have more exposure and marketability — and it is free. For these
types of services you'd pay $30 or more a month to
other sites that do not guarantee a fan base. MySpace
does not make any guarantees either, but at least
you're being wise and not throwing money into the
unknown.

Take my advice, for whatever it's worth. I first signed up in June of '05. I thought I could leave the site on autopilot and people would come. Wrong move. Like anything in the marketing world, you must be active! From June 'till I got up to speed in January, only 50 people saw my site and listened to my music.

When I became active by simply logging in every other day, adding friends and meeting people, my site took off. Presently, my site has been visited by 600-plus people who have listened to my music. MySpace is a great tool, but you still must make the effort to sell yourself responsibly and genuinely.

Darrel Kathan
Machines Gone Mad
www.myspace.com/machinesgonemad

General thoughts on MySpace as a promotion tool:

The "friend" and "comments" concepts of MySpace have made it brilliantly addictive and has attracted a great deal of young, energetic music lovers. You can easily approach strangers who may become great fans or even do work for you by doing photography at shows, participating on a street team, or just spreading the word.

Top MySpace marketing tips:

- Browse for friends in your area or the area you will be performing in.

- Read their profiles to find out if they have any "rules" about friend requests. If not, add 'em.

- If they accept, thank them by posting a comment or sending an IM. That way you're "showin' the love." If you send a friend request and they accept, it means more if you pay attention specifically to them.

- Don't be afraid to send a request to some-one if they don't specify any restrictions. People are often very flattered by your request and some are even nice!

- Whenever possible, try to follow up your friend request with a message that connects with them, like "Zoolander is my favorite movie, too!" or "Where did you get that cool background?"

- Stick with it. There are a lot of new people signing up every day who go there to net-work. Maybe not everyone wants to network with *you* but everyone wants to feel good and have a good time, and that's what you sell them, if they let you.

Biggest MySpace drawbacks:

It's the worst piece of programming I have ever seen. It's clunky and awkward at best, and downright useless at times.

If someone sends a friend request and it is declined, the requester does not get any response and their request just sits in their "pending requests." I have never let them sit long enough to know if they ever get removed.

I also hate that "people" and "bands" are in two separate spaces. If you browse for people you will not find any bands unless you go to the music section. Sometimes individual people are musicians, but if they want to include their music on their page, they are cast out into the music area. Unless that changes, never expect people to come looking for you if you are a band. You will have to go to them.

Additional MySpace thoughts:

Be careful. It's more addictive than crack.

Michael Ahlström
Violent Divine
www.myspace.com/theviolentdivine

General thoughts on MySpace as a promotion tool:

I think it's so great. It sort of sums up what I think is great about the Internet: It's one big community. Fans, bands and bizniz joined together. It's a complete revolution, just like MP3.com was in its heyday.

Top MySpace marketing tips:

- Invite people, but only those who it makes sense to invite. It's no use to gather just a mass of friends.

- Get personal. Talk to those friends. You will meet them on tour and they will become a great local asset to your band.

- Don't make a mess of your site. All these streaming features and extra graphics that are linked in will take an eon to load and people may miss what you're trying to accomplish. Keep it clean and effective.

Additional MySpace thoughts:

So far we have been very fortunate on MySpace. We got a record deal with Chavis Records. I'm currently talking to promoters and booking agencies to organize tours, radio stations, magazines. Our life as a band and the way we moved forward we owe a lot to our little spot on MySpace.

Chris Holmes
Lube
www.myspace.com/lubeband

General thoughts on MySpace as a promotion tool:

At first glance, MySpace looks like your typical college Internet gimmicky fad like Facebook.com or AIM. I fought off many suggestions from other bands/friends to put us on MySpace. "It seems cheesy," I commonly replied. That was until a sat down and looked at one of my friend's band's profile.

This thing is very clever! First, an individual creates a page with tons of info about themselves and invites their "Friends" to come look at it and comment on them. In our self-centered culture this is perfect. Who doesn't want everyone to 1) look at them 2) give them feedback and tell them they are great.

For bands, it covers a little more. Bands can make MySpace a one-stop place for everything that is their band. Most bands' web sites are not kept up to date, mostly because we are musicians, not web developers (well, most of us). MySpace solves this because it is easy to use and update.

We use our profile as an electronic press kit of sorts. It contains our streaming music, our bio, schedule, pictures, our blog, e-mail sign up, who we sound like /influences and *feedback from fans*. This allows fans to see what other people think about us and gives club owners a chance to see if our crowd is the right fit — or if we can even pull a crowd.

It's almost too perfect from a marketing standpoint. The only thing that would make it better would be to allow the sale of your MP3s for download from your profile. We have only been using MySpace since January 2006 and have had well over 1,800 views and 1,200 friends — many of whom are *new* fans. That is valuable marketing!

Top MySpace marketing tips:

- Find people in your area who you know or would like to show your band to ... and add them as your friends.

- Respond to your fans who contact you/leave comments. They will remember that you are "cool" and tell someone else about your music.

- Create separate sites for each of your band members. Remember, those people you went to high school with? They might search for you and not make fun of you for being in a band. My personal profile has been invaluable for showing those people that I *can* make a living playing music while they work some lame 9 to 5. Then they become a fan or supporter and add you as a friend.

- Seek out bands that have a similar type fan base. We are a community and we need each other to succeed.

- Invite your "friends" to tell their "friends" about you.

- Send your event invites to your fans/friends. (Does anyone know how to include all of your friends to be invited to an event without individually selecting each one to be entered on the list?)

- Bulletins! Don't send useless info, but *do* send out updates with your regular e-mail list updates. Have a new song on your profile? Send a bulletin.

- Log in regularly so that your fans/friends feel that they are interacting with you and that you are a part of something together.

- Send out thanks/comments when someone asks to be your friend. They have taken the time to seek you out.

- Don't spend too much time on MySpace and forget to practice!

Biggest MySpace drawbacks:

The server is slow! There are a ton of scammers/ spammers and creeps on there giving it a bad rap, thus scaring away good potential fans. Other than that, what drawbacks could there be to marketing yourself, in a professional manner, to 80 million potential fans?

Additional MySpace thoughts:

MySpace is a great tool and should be used along with the many other tools out there.

Catherine Duc
www.myspace.com/catherineduc

General thoughts on MySpace as a promotion tool:

MySpace is probably the largest and most active online community. For musicians wanting to gain targeted traffic, without the risks of spamming, this is an ideal site.

Top MySpace marketing tips:

- Find the MySpace pages of well-known artists that perform music similar to your music style. Invite them as your friend, and post a comment on their page. Pretty soon, you'll be getting invitations from their fans, who see your comment on the artist's page. You can also initiate your own invitations to fans of that artist.

- Join community groups that you're interested in (i.e., independent artists, Irish music, etc). You can then access a network of people with similar interests.

- Encourage your new friends on MySpace to use one of your songs as the default song on their page. You'll get more traffic if their friends like the song.

Biggest MySpace drawbacks:

Sometimes you may get unwanted messages/comments from certain people. You may also end up getting a lot of messages and comments that will take you some time to reply to — especially if you become quite popular. But then, that would be a good problem to have!

Craig Ferguson

www.myspace.com/craigfergusonmusic
www.myspace.com/erikjansonmusic
www.myspace.com/rootsaliveatroom5

General thoughts on MySpace as a promotion tool:

Yes, not only have I had success with MySpace as a "session musician" advertising my services and directing traffic to my web site, but one of my bands has also had lot of success with MySpace. The bottom line is that MySpace is an amazing tool to connect people that wouldn't otherwise be connected. I've received offers for gigs and session work from people I've never met and don't know how they found me.

Top MySpace marketing tips:

- This one is our best! For our band's residency in L.A. we created an alias and a whole separate page for the show. Our fictitious "host" is named "Rootsey Collings" and the page is called Roots Alive! at Room 5. We then started sending out individual e-mails to friends of our friends from Mr. Collings. (Note: we did not spam entire lists of people, we sent messages one by one.)

  We made our form letter fun, goofy, enjoyable and asked each person, "If you'll be my friend, well that would just make my day!" Needless to say, the results have been impressive.

- In the "about me" section, I've put "hot" links to other MySpace artists who I've done session work for. Often in return, they will put a "hot" link back to my page. It works!

- When the band I'm in (Erik Janson) has an out-of-town show, we'll search in that city for profiles that have matching influences. For example, if we sound like Taj Mahal, we'll enter "Taj Mahal" in the city we're playing and profiles of people who like his music with come up. Then we'll kindly e-mail them and let them know about our show based on that fact that we both like the same artists.

James Frey
Blue Island Tribe
www.myspcae.com/blueislandtribe

General thoughts on MySpace as a promotion tool:

MySpace levels the playing field for indies to compete with major label acts.

Top MySpace marketing tips:

- When I send out bulletins for shows or newsletters, I always put at the end of my message, "If you know of any venues, festivals, parties or bands that you think would fit the Blue Island Tribe, let us know." This has become a great success for booking in markets that I have not even thought about breaking into.

- Another great marketing idea: Every time we add 500 new friends to our MySpace, we throw a response contest. We usually give away 5 to 10 prize packs including CDs, stickers and posters. I usually put a time limit for response so we are not getting responses two months down the road. People will do just about anything to get free stuff.

- When inviting friends, I will choose the zip codes of the cities we will be playing in. I will then try to invite at least 100 friends to join our MySpace account. I will usually do this about one month before we play there. This gives that market a chance to soak up our music so when they come to our show they will be singing our songs. Not to mention, this helps with merch sales as well.

Biggest MySpace drawbacks:

The biggest drawback I can think of is that every band on MySpace is promoting itself way too much. Granted, it is good to promote yourself, but if you send newsletters and show invites every single day, you are saturating the market, thus ruining the experience. Who takes the time to open 40 invites a day to a place where you are not going to be for the next five years?

Nick Mitchell
Endless Blue
www.myspace.com/endlessblue

General thoughts on MySpace as a promotion tool:

MySpace is the new MP3.com. It's the most powerful free tool out there today. It's actually a more powerful tool than the "old school" MP3.com in that it's more of a "hangout," making it easier to get to potential fans.

Top MySpace marketing tips:

- It's not the quantity of friends you have, it's the quality of friends. I have seen plenty of bands that have 2,000 friends, but have only 250 plays. That means that yes, they are making "friends," but no one is really taking the time to listen. It's better to have a smaller number of friends that you truly connect with and talk to.

- Always, always, always leave a comment for anyone who adds you as a friend. This is essentially the way you get known — people visiting others' spaces scan through the comments and look at who's posting, then check them out. It's okay to link a small banner image in the comment, just be thoughtful about it.

It is also very, very important to actually read your new friend's space and comment something personal about them, rather than blindly adding "Thx for the add!" This will open up a connection between you and the fan, and it will make them more likely to like you.

- Make sure and stop by your friends' spaces and leave comments every so often so they don't forget about you. Again, fight the urge to post a form message. Make it personal. This will keep the friendships alive. This is especially important for fans.

Biggest MySpace drawbacks:

It's a huge time investment to make sure you promote the "right" way. It can be a little daunting to have 25 friend requests that you need to respond to on a personal basis, and it can quickly become a time drain. Also, in a lot of ways, you won't see a huge return on your time investment. It's a bits and pieces kind of situation, so it can be a bit frustrating at times.

Andrew Gilpin
Ebony & Ivory
www.myspace.com/ebonyandivoryduo

General thoughts on MySpace as a promotion tool:

Although I'm relatively new to MySpace, I've found it invaluable in finding fans, other musicians, etc. These are people it would have been difficult to reach any other way, given our geographical separation.

Top MySpace marketing tips:

- **Targeted messaging**. First of all, I search MySpace profiles to find people who like our kind of music. Fans of artists who have influenced our sound will likely enjoy our music as well. Then I send an introductory message introducing our group and inviting them to visit our profile page. Approximately one in three people have responded by sending friend requests and/or giving us positive feedback.

  I've also tried random messaging (writing to "cool new people," etc.) but the targeted approach seems to be the most effective.

- **Statistic scraping**. After playing around with MySpace for a while, I thought, "Wouldn't it be cool if I could have my

MySpace statistics (number of friends and profile views) show up on my group's web site?" After searching the Net for something to help me accomplish this, and finding nothing, I ended up writing a PHP script of my own.

If you visit our home page (www.ebonyand ivory.ca), on the sidebar there's a link to our MySpace profile, along with our latest number of friends and profile views. As far as I can tell, nobody else has written a script to display MySpace statistics on an external web page. I would be happy to share this script with anyone who wants it.

- **Cross-linking**. When you visit our home page (www.ebonyandivory.ca), on the sidebar there's a link to our MySpace profile. And, of course, there's a link to our band's web site on our MySpace profile. This, combined with up-to-the-second statistics, generates more page views for both sites.

- **Maintenance**. I think the most important factor in relationships with fans is maintaining them! Especially with a site like MySpace, which has people on 24/7, it's very important to respond to comments, deal with friend requests, etc., in a timely manner.

Biggest MySpace drawbacks:

The first thing that comes to mind is that the general kind of music that most people seem to like is singer/songwriter pop/rock. We're an instrumental jazz-fusion group, so I think we have a greater challenge in getting our music out there. On the other hand, one of our most effusive comments was from a local metal band that just loves our stuff, so you just never know!

Additional MySpace thoughts:

I have found MySpace to be a friendly place overall. I haven't been flamed (yet!) and the response to our music has been very positive.

Katie McGowan
Promotion for **Submerse**
www.myspace.com/submerse

General thoughts on MySpace as a promotion tool:

It's a fantastic way to gain exposure to a new audience, show yourself off to A&R, and even book shows! But as always, it should be used with other forms of promotion.

Top MySpace marketing tips:

- Post a comment for everybody who accepts you as a friend. Try to make them personal. Why would a fan want a comment that's simply a flier plugging you to others? MySpace is about communication, so use it to communicate with your fans. If people see you care, they're more interested. Nobody wants to stay in touch with an advert!

- Competitions. Everybody loves a competition and it's so simple to get fans involved on MySpace. Competitions for merch, free tickets, even a place in your MySpace "Top 8" have gone down very well for Submerse and have been used to spread the word of the band.

  One example we used recently: Fans had the chance to win a DVD. All fans had to do was add Submerse to their Top 8 (there's the boring but effective promo bit) then visit our profile and leave a message saying what band member they'd take out on Valentine's Day (the fun bit that got the fans involved, talking about the band, etc.). Top answers won DVDs.

- The fans there can act as a street team. If you want to win an online vote, let them know. If you have a short-notice gig, post it as a bulletin. We offer stickers and extra bits and pieces to anybody who puts up the Submerse banner or video on their own MySpace profile.

- There are music forums on MySpace that are very genre specific. Make sure you use them.

- Networking with other bands similar to you and encouraging promotion ("I'll plug you if you plug me") works pretty well too. Similarly, many clothing and print companies on there are interested in working with bands that have a strong fan base. Cross-promotion can be really effective, even online!

- Don't be afraid to mention your merch and special offers to MySpace fans. We actually sell ours via the site using PayPal. It's helped raise tour funds.

- Use MySpace for peer-to-peer marketing. Encourage fans to download a sample track or full MP3 and spread it around.

- Make your page stand out. Pages that look slightly different from the norm keep surfers for longer. We've changed ours with colors and the addition of a video.

- Don't be afraid to mention that you're on MySpace at shows or add it to the bottom of fliers. Many people out there use it. The more fans who add you, the bigger audience you go out to. Submerse had no Internet access during last year's Canadian tour, but because they mentioned MySpace at their shows, fans went home, added the band and they now stay in touch. Due to fans adding the band, their Canadian fan base has spread since the tour.

Biggest MySpace drawbacks:

The errors — but what can you expect from a free service? At times gig info posted in bulletins goes to fans who live in different countries, which must be annoying for fans. We've tried to rectify this by posting locations in our bulletin titles.

At times it's hard to define how effective MySpace marketing is because right now there are no statistics on the pages. Don't judge your friend's list as your "fan list" because, at the end of the day, you might never see some of those people at a show of yours. Sometimes, it can be quite time-consuming to respond to the fan requests.

Although MySpace is great, don't spend hours a day on there when you could be using that time to promote your band via other popular mediums. It worries me that some bands use it alone for promotions simply because it reaches a wide audience. MySpace should always be used in conjunction with other forms of promo.

Additional MySpace thoughts:

At any time MySpace may start charging, shut down, or you may have an error and lose your list of fans. Bands should think about what they've done to ensure they stay in touch with their fans if this happens. Mailing lists, frequent mentions of their own web sites and forums, and setting up street teams are all good ways of keeping your fans involved.

It shouldn't be about how big your fan list looks. What's more important is that you can convert those fans into ticket buyers, CD sales and promoters. If you go around adding everybody, chances are they'll listen to you once and never again. By all means, use these methods to promote yourself but don't go adding random people. That is time consuming and ineffective. "If you build it, they will come." Believe me, industry people can tell who the "friend adders" are!

Be sure to use the knowledge of fans in other areas/ countries. After all, they'll know about the local press (radio/mags/web sites/TV), what venues are great for bands, and even suggestions of bands you could gig-swap with.

And let's not forget they'll know what independent

record stores will stock new CDs. MySpace is a fantastic tool for setting up tours and grassroots promotions, providing you take full advantage of what it has to offer.

Also, feel free to check out www.ukbands.net. It's a portal for bands that want to play the UK. Everybody is welcome — fans, bands, promoters, venues, photographers. It's free to use and has brand new opportunities for bands daily.

Kate and Kacey Coppola

www.myspace.com/kateandkaceycoppola

General thoughts on MySpace as a promotion tool:

MySpace is an amazing new tool for musicians to use in promoting absolutely any type of music because it is a one-stop site for everything that an independent artist needs: other musicians to play with, open for, and ask to open for you; a *giant* pool of potential new fans, clubs and coffee shops looking for new acts to book; record label interest; indie radio stations looking for great new songs to add to their playlists … the list goes on and on!

Top MySpace marketing tips:

- Have a slam-dunk profile picture. Sad to say, but most people see before they look, and in turn *hear*. To attract more potential fans to your site, you *have* to get them interested based on visual alone. But we mean *classy* visual. For musicians, that's either a dynamite shot that isn't like every other typical band shot, or even a really creative logo or visually stunning picture that can wrap around what your music is all about. After you get them to come and look a little deeper, you reel 'em in with your amazing and undeniable music. The point is to drive traffic to your site, and then let the art speak for you.

- For as long as you can, try to respond to everyone who asks to be your friend or writes you a message. It's hard and time consuming ... but on numerous occasions, just by writing back — creating that line of personal communication — and thanking someone for taking the time to listen and comment, add your act, etc, we have gotten e-mail addresses for our mailing list, questions regarding how to get a hold of our CD, and several new fans out to shows.

The extra personal contact is a luxury that these people don't get with the big-time musicians they already love. And they are so grateful to you for writing them back — they can't believe it! It makes them bold enough to ask for that CD, to tell you they're coming to a show, to want to be on your mailing list. Plus, it makes it even better for us because we get to know new people, we get to have conversations about our music with complete strangers — we find out what it is about our art that speaks to people. It's a gold mine of information that will make you a better writer, a better musician, and a better person.

- Join groups that either reflect the type of music you make, have members that match your target fan profile, or just interest you in general. This is a much better way to make yourself known to potential fans than by randomly asking every new profile you come across to add your band. That is like catching a fly with chopsticks — a nice idea, but very hard to do.

Most people, if they don't know you or your music, just get annoyed with tons of new bands/acts pestering them with adds all the time. You have to go to them, make them think they found *you*. You can do this by joining legit groups and getting your profile pic (see our first tip) out there. If you seem interested in what your potential new fan is interested in, you have a much better chance of actually making a new fan.

For example, we joined the Boulder Acoustic

Music Group for two reasons: 1) We are from Colorado, and our music reflects that rootsy feel of the Rocky Mountains, and 2) We play acoustic music. By joining that group, we have gotten a lot of traffic to our site from Colorado music fans who (what a concept!) love acoustic music. Done. New fans and we didn't even have to bully them into becoming fans!

Biggest MySpace drawbacks:

Like we said above, the whole idea of quantity over quality doesn't benefit any act. The number of "friends" you have on MySpace means nothing if most of these people just added you because you asked, and they don't really have a vested interest in who you are or what kind of music you make. If they don't remember you the next time they see your picture or hear your music, then they aren't really your "friend."

The quality of your "friends," though? That is the most important part. Are these friends going to return to your page? Are they going to read your bulletins? Are they going to buy your CD? Join your mailing list? Read your blogs? You want friends who are "fans" ... otherwise, you're just wasting your time. And that is a precious commodity.

Ant Boogie
Collective Hallucination

www.myspace.com/antboogie1
www.myspace.com/collectivehallucination

General thoughts on MySpace as a promotion tool:

I love using MySpace as a promotional tool because I can reach more people in my city alone who will take time to listen to my band, read my blogs, and support me than I can through radio advertising or print media. I would rather reach 100 people who are gonna support my band than reach one million who couldn't care less.

Top MySpace marketing tips:

- I've developed personal relationships with just about everyone on both the Collective Hallucination and Ant Boogie pages. I get to know them instead of just adding someone and saying, "Hey check out my music." I send e-mails and get to know everyone on my page better. Some of them I've actually exchanged phone numbers and ideas with. Many of them I now consider family. We hang out and I know their families, etc.

- I've run contests on MySpace and I've given away merchandise just to get the name and the "brand" out there. I encourage people who come see us to turn their friends on to us. And 9 times out of 10, they do. Their friends get turned on to us and they, in turn, turn others on to us.

- I recently e-mailed a number of people and encouraged them to download our song "Somebody The '05 Remix," and they did. Upon listening to the song and getting that cozy "soul" feeling that CH has become known for, many people purchased the Collective Hallucination CD. I sold 25 CDs in one month and we didn't have a single performance! Out of that 25, more than half were sold because of MySpace.

- I think this is probably the most important thing I've done since joining My Space: I've met other artists and bands in my area and we've teamed up more than once this year to put on concerts and shows. And because of that, not only has my fan base grown, but so has the other bands'.

Also, I've gotten a lot of requests from other artists to write music or lyrics for them and to produce their CDs. So MySpace has been a godsend for me. Recently I jammed on stage with Prince and Tamar, and that just sent my "approval rating" through the roof. I even sold some CDs at the Tamar (featuring Prince) concert. Imagine that!

Biggest MySpace drawbacks:

I don't see any drawbacks. I know there are other artists on MySpace, including major label acts, who are trying to get the same attention we indie artists are working for. It makes me work harder and smarter. Like I said before, since I take a personal approach to all of the people on my friends list, it's been a real cool experience.

Additional MySpace thoughts:

You can't sleep on your dream. When others are awake working and you're sleeping, that puts them 10 steps closer to where you're trying to be. This music business is a 24/7 job and if you take too many breaks, you end up broke.

Elizabeth Mauban
Promotion for **Courage Under Chaos, Evening With Emily, They Walk On Skeletons, Eleven Bravo,** and **TC the Band**
www.myspace.com/courageunderchaos
www.myspace.com/eveningwithemily
www.myspace.com/theywalkonskeletons
www.myspace.com/elevenbravo
www.myspace.com/tctheband

General thoughts on MySpace as a promotion tool:

MySpace is definitely a good idea if you're trying to target an age group of maybe 13 to 23. MySpace is very popular among young people.

Top MySpace marketing tips:

- To gain more friends, a suggestion is to already know people on MySpace who can help promote you. Have banners and buttons available on your page so they can pass it around to spread the word.

- Never use "whore trains" or any such thing (which are messages sent to all MySpace friends on a bulletin board that has "add me" blurbs about a band or a person.) Yes, some people add off of those, but they most likely just want their number of friends to go up. You want real fans who care about you, so a number hunter isn't going to cut it.

- Do have short (or at least clear and easy to read) information. Not too many people are going to sit through a whole page of some-thing like a band bio if it's too long or hard to read.

- Have pictures and songs up. Pictures of live shows or just goofing off are good. Anything to give fans and MySpacers a sense of who you are. Music ... well, people want to know what you sound like before running off and telling everyone about you.

- A "pimped out" page is always nice to look at. It shows you put time and effort into reaching fans.

- Leaving personal comments. For some reason, comments are so important to people that they spam bulletins telling you to leave them comments. Some bands leave picture comments, such as a picture of the band and the message "Thanks for being our friend." Although that boosts their comments, it's not very personal.

  This is something I stress to my boys in the bands a lot: Telling people "happy birthday" or "thanks for coming out to the show" or pointing out something on their page ... that will be remembered and show you're not just another MySpace band. It shows you care about your fans.

- Keep an UPDATED list of upcoming shows. Let fans know when they can come see you play.

Biggest MySpace drawbacks:

- Some people dislike MySpace and will refuse to listen because you are "another MySpace sell out."

- MySpace also has many technological problems and is down quite a bit so the public won't always be able to see your page.

- It is also losing popularity to the school-based Facebook.com, which doesn't do much for music.

- People wanting to help spread the word to schools may not have success because MySpace is blocked by many schools.

Additional MySpace thoughts:

I have a MySpace profile and all the bands I promote do as well. We are all in the high school range and MySpace is *so* popular with us and all our friends. Along with a MySpace page, a separate web site should also be available, for viewing in school. That may sound funny, but it is true.

Bob Oedy
Glue Gun, The Grim
www.myspace.com/glugun

www.myspace.com/thegrimlive

General thoughts on MySpace as a promotion tool:

MySpace is a godsend for independent artists. It's free! What could be better? It's also so easy to use. The problem is most people either don't know how to get the most out of it or they just let it linger and ... well, you know how that goes.

Top MySpace marketing tips:

- If a picture is worth a thousand words than load up on pictures. Glue Gun has a song entitled "Eva's Got a Mohawk," so our default photo is a chick with a mohawk. It's like a magnet for punk rockers, which is exactly what our fan base is. The first thing you should do is post a photo.

- We bought four copies of the MySpace album, which allows you to post four extra pictures per profile. You need to fill out the card inside and mail it. I hear there's some way to hack the site and do it for free but ... we might be a punk band, but with integrity.

- When you accept someone new as a friend, go to their profile and request to be added to all their friends' lists. Friends almost always share interests in the same kinds of music.

- Each band member should have their own site (with photos). Even if they don't care for the Web, make them. Do it for them. Answer their mail. It will lead people to the band site.

- The best feature on MySpace is the "Top 8." Make people work for it. This is where the "fans" belong. If they don't post comments, bump them. Tell them you just bumped them and why. In fact, tell everyone this is a competition. I guarantee they will start posting comments.

Additional MySpace thoughts:

I hate when bands post a message every day. Okay, I know your band's name but you're so obnoxious I will never go to see you, and don't think for a second I will recommend you to my friends.

People often post disgusting images in the comments section. I recommend you check them often and hit delete.

Renee Sebastian
www.myspace.com/reneesebastian

General thoughts on MySpace as a promotion tool:

In my opinion, MySpace, when used intelligently as a targeted marketing tool, can be very beneficial to the self-promoting musician. The problem is, how does one begin to go through the massive amount of "friends"? It is quite easy to fall victim to one's desire to be the most popular "friend" out there (who, of course, is Tom). After all, who wants to admit they only have a handful of friends, let alone publicize it?

I was listening to the radio one night. The DJ encouraged MySpace users to call in to promote their profiles. The DJ proceeded to question them on the number of friends they have. One caller said he had only 47 friends and the DJ simply hung up on the guy and said, "He's a loser." Musicians may deny it, but I bet they look at other artist's profiles and check how many fans they have. Hell, I've done it.

Competition is good, but MySpace is just a data mining solution. It is you, the user/musician, that is the brains behind it. You must know how to use it as a marketing, promotion, and networking tool. If you don't go the extra mile and make sense out of all this information, what you may have could very well be just a whole lot of nothing.

Top MySpace marketing tips:

- **Make Valuable Friends**. Every successful
  marketing campaign begins with a clear
  understanding of the target audience.
  MySpace allows all profilers to list their
  interests, age, college education, music
  interests, etc. By being patient and reading
  through this information, you'll have a good
  chance of adding a friend that could very
  well be a real fan. Forget about the "friends
  counter." It's not about having 10,000-plus
  friends. It's about having 100 true fans who
  are waiting for you to drop that record. I
  typically narrow my friend searches based
  on interests and keywords.

- **Make Intelligent Associations**. I think
  joining the right MySpace group can be
  another way to interact with potential fans.
  I've actually done this more at MyTribe.com
  and TagWorld.com, but the same can be
  used at MySpace. It's a great way to get
  feedback, hear perspective, and network
  with other artists. I actually got two book-
  ings in NYC and one in St. Louis at very
  good venues — all from having a MySpace
  profile. It's pretty encouraging when you get
  a message requesting for you to perform at
  their venue.

- **Use the Tools**. Everyone loves a pretty package. Customize your profile page. It sets you apart. However, I hate pages that take a long time to load. I don't use the blog and calendar as much in MySpace because I have an account with Blogger and a Sonicbids calendar that I can embed in my profile. However, I understand that other musicians get more hits because of what they write on their blogs. I also embed a YouTube.com video into my profile and upload songs into their audio player. I optimize all objects I embed so that people won't get turned off waiting for my page to show up.

- **Post a Comment, Don't Message**. As a musician, I get a lot of messages from friends making remarks about my music. I always respond to them but not by replying to the message. I go to their profiles and post a *personal* comment. This obviously increases your visibility plus it may strike curiosity with other potential fans.

- **Bulletin and Event Away?** As much as possible, I only send my bulletins and events to the right target fans for a given location. However, MySpace narrow searches are sometimes buggy and so, unfortunately, I'm forced to blast an event announcement. Ideally, avoid reaching out to friends who may not benefit from your bulletin or event announcement. Believe it or not, I've been surprised by MySpace friends actually showing up at my gigs. I'm in NYC right now and two weeks ago, I didn't have a clue who to invite to my performances. I reached out to MySpace friends in the NYC/NJ area and am quite pleased to find that MySpace friends are genuinely fans. Of course, this would only work if you've targeted the right friends in the first place per my first point earlier.

Biggest MySpace drawbacks:

I haven't experienced any drawbacks perhaps because I understand the power and limitations of this marketing tool. My expectations are realistic.

Jennifer Richman
www.myspace.com/jenniferrichman

General thoughts on MySpace as a promotion tool:

It is a great promotional tool. Very smart and very cost effective. You can reach international fans that normally would be untouchable by other indie means.

Top MySpace marketing tips:

- I've compared my music to that of other known artists and was very specific. One person bought a CD just based on the description because she likes all of the artists mentioned.

- Spend time on MySpace adding friends and keep in touch with them. It brings you in reach and is very appreciated by fans.

- Contacts can be made easily on MySpace. I've been on several podcasts because of MySpace.

Biggest MySpace drawbacks:

It takes a lot of time and it interferes with practice, daily routines, sleep, etc.

Additional MySpace thoughts:

We are lucky to have sites like MySpace at this day and time. I think it will change many aspects of the music business because it opens up people's eyes to just how much great indie music is out there.

Don Harrison
Baytown Underground

http://www.myspace.com/baytownunderground

Top MySpace marketing tips:

I use MySpace to promote BaytownUnderground.com. My first step was completing the profile questions with a proper answer while plugging my site address in every section. I change it up every now and then to keep it interesting. When I blog I also post a bulletin on the subject with a reference to the blog and to my site. Also, your friends list and favorites act as a mailing list of sorts. I am also able to find content for my site by scouring blogs and posts.

I always message each band to let them know they are on the front page of my site. The classifieds and forums are a bonus when marketing.

Biggest MySpace drawbacks:

The biggest drawback is the tremendous number of people posting at the same time. It seems your bulletin is lost in a sea of meaningless bullshit at times.

Additional MySpace thoughts:

I find it easy to market myself because it's a laid-back atmosphere and I am able to talk to the musicians like we would talk if we met in a club.

John Pippus

www.myspace.com/johnpippus

General thoughts on MySpace as a promotion tool:

My experience is that it's a great place to meet fellow songwriters/performers to talk about songwriting, performing, and industry tips. In terms of getting people out to gigs, I've had limited success. I don't have a CD for sale at this point, so others would have to address that aspect. Lately I've become frustrated with the number of requests for "adds" from various wannabe rock stars and then, when I add them, I never hear from them. It's like I'm supposed to go and hear how fabulous their tunes are and post a comment to that effect and that's the end of it.

MySpace is a grassroots effort. Even the originator, Tom, tries to keep it on a "friendly" level. I don't think the term "friend" was chosen lightly. And I am getting tired of being a one-way friend. In frustration, I've decided — for now at least — to cap my friend list to 100 people. I add one, but take away one who has not demonstrated any friendly good manners.

Top MySpace marketing tips:

- Do not ever say "thanks for the add." That is the most overused cliché on MySpace.

- Don't have some flack run your site. Run it

yourself or go find some other forum where you can get your message out.

- Respond. Initiate. Listen. Communicate. MySpace is, or should be, a two-way street. Would you want a friend who never talked to you and just expected you to talk to them? Sure, it's time-consuming. But so is friendship.

What works for me in terms of reaching fans/friends is:

- Posting decent songs
- Posting interesting and useful blogs
- Posting original comments on other people's profiles

Biggest MySpace drawbacks:

It's time-consuming ... and addictive.

Menios Symeon
www.myspace.com/meniossymeon

General thoughts on MySpace as a promotion tool:

It is misused by some people thinking that adding as many friends as possible is the key to success. For me, MySpace is not a race for who's most popular, but a way to share your music and make people happier by listening to it.

Also, MySpace is a purely Western music promotion tool. How many times have you seen a foreign band being showcased as "new cool people"? How many times has a foreign band been promoted heavily on the front page of MySpace?

Top MySpace marketing tips:

I have three, but first consider this: The number one marketing tool in music is music itself. Let's not forget that. No need to explain further, but I think good music is like water running free. You can't stop it from free flowing into people's music collection. Three tips:

- Always stay logged in. That way, you will be shown on the first page when someone searches for people online in your area.

- Keep in close touch as much as you can with friends and fans. Be active as much as possible. Keep your blog running with inter-esting stuff like videos from your shows, your everyday life on the road and with the band, and funny and silly things happening along the way. Share experiences, sorrows and happy moments. Connect. This will create traffic and draw attention to you — if you have something worthy to say or sing, that is. Don't shout and insult people's personalities. Respect yourself. Others will respect you.

- Be yourself and nobody else. Even if that costs you. Don't go spamming everyone, thinking that more friends means more fans. Let's be frank ... a MySpace friend is not the only way to define a real fan.

Biggest MySpace drawbacks:

My space regularly has errors and programming issues, which is understandable, but always unwelcome. MySpace is not always a place for friends. Many people go online just to waste other people's time and nerves, just to make a fool of themselves.

Joseph Powell
Helix Eternal
www.myspace.com/helixeternal

General thoughts on MySpace as a promotion tool:

It's a great way to network with other musicians, to get the word out for your shows or releases, and to find a fan base for your music.

Top MySpace marketing tips:

- Find similar artists to your own music and

send out mass messages to people on their friends lists. Chances are they will be interested in what you have to offer if they are into another artist of the same genre.

- Get your friends to send out the word for you (like a web version of a street team)

- Post the link to your MySpace page everywhere you possibly can. It's like fishing for listeners, and you'll probably hook a few.

Biggest MySpace drawbacks:

A lot of people don't take MySpace seriously because many artist pages have been set up by rabid teenage fans.

Andrea Gerak

www.myspace.com/gerakandrea

General thoughts on MySpace as a promotion tool:

I have been on MySpace for only six weeks or so, but this is what I've got out of it so far:

- No sales yet. I have to figure out what to do better and how.

- New fans who haven't heard me before —

and hey, as I go into some little talk with them, I find out that one of them is working in a CD shop, another one would *love* to hear me sing live and now is looking around to get me some gigs in his country, another one who is living on the other side of the world used to be my big love when I was 12, and so on.

- Great comments that I can use in my general promotion. It's good to monitor what people like about me. So I use MySpace as a kind of marketing survey, and it's also good for an extra self-confidence boost.

- Musician connections — the best thing so far. I got to know musicians who are real stars in the country where I am from, but I am not living there at the moment, and they are promoting me on their channels; somebody else who is now organizing a gig for me in his town in another country; several fantastic musicians who would like to work with me, which is absolutely great. A record company just contacted me: some of their artists, who are Grammy-winning names that I used to only dream about working with, are interested in working with me.

Top MySpace marketing tips:

- Be a *real* person. When I send a friend request to someone, first I check out who that person is and send a message along with the request. From that, they can see that it is not some automated add, but I want *them* as friends. This way, my requests are more effective, more people accept it than when I just shoot one to people in a targeted group.

- Also, when I get a request, I check out each page, if necessary, and even ask the person why they want me as a friend, and decide whether I'd like them around me or not. I cool-heartedly deny jerks — they shouldn't mess up my space! To this point, I try to be interest*ed* in people, rather than be interest-*ing* myself.

Of course, I am anyway interested and want to show what I've got, but I don't need to make them feel that they are only "one little pebble" and I am the "star." That wouldn't lead anywhere. They are all unique individuals, and if treated as such, they are grateful! Communication is a two-way thing, and if I'm not interested in what they want to communicate, why would I expect the same from them?

- It goes best when I myself feel good about being on MySpace and am using it as a marketing tool for my things. When I sit down to the computer and I am excited to see what's going on with this or that friend of mine, how many new friends I've gotten since the last time, how do people like my songs ... I feel creative and want to share my good news with everyone, or I really have fun checking out profiles, etc. — than I get many more friends and comments.

- Also, when writing comments to others, I feel that by putting a link to my web site through my cool picture, I basically offer them something nice. People seem to receive the vibes and respond to it by adding me. But when I sit there trying to push up the numbers, or have a bad consciousness about being pushy advertising my own stuff ... then I better stand up from the computer and do something else. Keep the spirits up. That works.

- Finding targeted groups and forums where people will be interested in my stuff. As I am Hungarian, my first choices were Hungarian groups. Sometimes I get involved in a topic or two, and it's also great to post bulletins to these groups. Now, when my web site has visitors from 90 countries, I get the most from Hungary.

Additional MySpace thoughts:

- I don't know yet what my chances are to get well-known on MySpace with my music, personality and ethical promotion efforts. There are artists who use services whereby they can send out hundreds of friend requests or comments a day with an automatic program they can buy for 50 bucks. You can choose, for example, groups where you want to send friend requests to each member with one click. Of course, you will get all kinds of assholes as well, but if one goes only for the numbers, that doesn't matter.

- MySpace is only one channel. This general principle I've learned holds true: The important thing is to give to people — only *then* will something come back to you, and not always from where you expect it. Sending friend requests, comments, answering messages on MySpace, showing your presence (on MySpace and elsewhere) will result in web site visitors and more. But the point is to *give out* and not just take in.

- Finally, MySpace is only what you make of it. If you think you'll sell all your stuff there, you probably will. If you think you'll get good connections, you will. If you think it's a meaningless, robotic, fake community ...

there you go. It all depends on your state of mind and how you approach it.

Denis Gauthier
theBetween
www.myspace.com/thebetween

General thoughts on MySpace as a promotion tool:

Great stuff ... better if you don't have to do the work ... I'm too busy to do everything at once.

Top MySpace marketing tips:

This is what I did: The first few months I just left it alone because I didn't have the time to get it all running. Then someone was very interested in what we are doing, added us and left a positive comment. So I asked her if she wanted to run our MySpace page as a fan site. She took it over and started adding tons of people. She took over the design and everything. All for some merch (CDs and such). All I had to do was watch and monitor. I even advertised it to our fans as our first "fan site."

I'm about to ask her to do phase two of the adding. All the adds happened as soon as I got her on the job, although it's not much right now, this all happened very recently and is snowballing as I write this.

Michael Heppler
EYE9D

www.myspace.com/eye9d

General thoughts on MySpace as a promotion tool:

It's an incredibly easy tool for networking and promoting. It couldn't be easier to find individuals in your area with the same interests, unless you have a hookup with the FBI.

Top MySpace marketing tips:

- **Giveaways.** Give fans something for their time and effort. Give away tickets to shows, CDs, T-shirts. There isn't a better way to get someone's attention then giving them something for nothing.

- **Use graphics.** Nothing attracts the eye like a sharp photo or graphic to go along with your message. But nothing too cheesy. Leave the artwork to the professionals! Otherwise, it could have the opposite effect.

- **New content.** Keep your profile fresh by updating it regularly. Not every band can update their profile every day, but your fans are on there every day (or so you hope). They *won't* return regularly if the same content is up there day after day.

Additional MySpace thoughts:

Don't abuse the bulletin board! Can I say that again in caps? DON'T ABUSE THE BULLETIN BOARD! No one is going to click on your posts if they are constantly filled with polls, jokes, "add my friend" requests, etc. Use it to promote your shows, record releases, give-aways, news, etc. If you give your fans something of value, they will continue to pay attention to you. Let their friends post all the junk that fills the bulletin board, only to be ignored.

I used to think that MySpace was too much of a "teenage girl" kind of web site — some place to go online, e-mail, chat with friends, and share pictures of your favorite MTV pop stars. That is why I was so late to get my profile on there. I was late in the game and now I am trying to play catch up. Even if it is partially true about MySpace being a "teen-age girl" kind of site, you have to admit, wherever there are teen-age girls, there are teen-age boys. And if you are doing all-ages shows, there is no better place to promote to that audience.

Eric Acevedo
DUO
www.myspace.com/duochicago

General thoughts on MySpace as a promotion tool:

MySpace is definitely an industry tool and is a great way to connect with fans, other artists, and industry people. The MySpace music account is great how it lets you upload four songs on the site for download and listening.

Top MySpace marketing tips:

- Searching your friends/related artists/local artists and DJs, and adding their friends that you feel would be good connections to have, or good people to view your site.

- Answering every message possible from your fans. And controlling your comments by responding.

- Having banners, images, links, etc., and a good color scheme.

Roy Al Rendahl
Poppermost
www.myspace.com/poppermost

Top MySpace marketing tips:

Here is a tip that seems real obvious now, but it took a while for it to hit us. Put a song of yours on MySpace with the name of someone in the title (or it could be something like a hobby or place or thing).

We put up our song "Erika," then did a search for that name. You can do this for a name or whatever the song title is. From the results that come up, send them add requests and/or messages about your band and the song with their name. Suggest that they add the song to play on their page. It's probably worth checking to make sure that they actually might like your kind of music first though.

In our case, there are over 4,000 pages of results for the name "Erika." And you can narrow the search to certain zip codes or countries if you want. We put some Erikas in our Top 8 who are (or were) playing our "Erika."

Additional MySpace thoughts:

Basically, make hay while the sun shines. I get the feeling that MySpace is having a hard time keeping up with its growth rate. Make the most of MySpace while it is still working and is still free, and if it stays that way, so much the better.

A drawback of MySpace is that when I'm looking for appropriate people or companies to add, I just can't stop. I find more on each page that I go to.

49 More Places to Network, Attract Fans, Post MP3s and Videos, Create Podcasts, and More

MySpace is obviously the biggest of the social networking sites. But there are others — many others that you could potentially use to increase your level of exposure.

Sites That Cater to Musicians Specifically

Artist Now
www.artistnow.com

Download.com Music
(the company that purchased MP3.com)
music.download.com

Garage Band
www.garageband.com

Odeo
www.odeo.com

Pure Volume
www.purevolume.com

Sound Click
www.soundclick.com

Tag World
www.tagworld.com

Ultimate Band List
www.ubl.com

General Social Networking Sites

Buzznet
www.buzznet.com

Face Book
www.facebook.com

Face Party
www.faceparty.com

Friendster
www.friendster.com

Linked In
www.linkedin.com

Meet Up
www.meetup.com

MSN Spaces
spaces.msn.com

My Yearbook
www.myyearbook.com

Orkut
www.orkut.com

Passado
www.passado.com

Profile Heaven
www.profileheaven.com

Tribe
www.tribe.net

Xanga
www.xanga.com

Yahoo! 360
360.yahoo.com

Video Hosting Sites

One of the newest trends are sites that allow you to host and share your videos for free. There are now dozens of them, inlcuding the following:

Castpost
www.castpost.com

Daily Motion
www.dailymotion.com

Eyespot
www.eyespot.com

Google Video
video.google.com

Grouper
www.grouper.com

Home Movie
www.homemovie.com

iFilm
www.ifilm.com

Jumpcut
www.jumpcut.com

Meta Cafe
www.metacafe.com

Photo Bucket
www.photobucket.com

Put File
www.putfile.com

Simple Star
www.simplestar.com

Stickam
www.stickam.com

Streamload
www.streamload.com

Video Egg
www.videoegg.com

Vimeo
www.vimeo.com

Vmix
www.vmix.com

Vsocial
www.vsocial.com

You Tube
www.youtube.com

Zippy Videos
www.zippyvideos.com

Photo Sharing Sites

Flickr
www.flickr.com

Slide
www.slide.com

Zorpia
www.zorpia.com

And here are four more interesting sites you may be able to use to connect with others:

43 Things
www.43things.com

del.icio.us
del.icio.us

Now Public
www.nowpublic.com

Squidoo
www.squidoo.com

Final Thoughts on Using MySpace to Promote Your Music

Keep this in mind: Success on MySpace (or any of the new interactive networking sites) isn't about the features and the technology *per se*. It's about connecting with people — as the site's motto says, it's "a place for friends." So stay focused on making friends and turning friends into fans who then talk you up to their friends, etc.

All of the MySpace music success stories you've read about have one thing in common: They're all about the ping-pong effect. It's not just you directly telling 100,000 people how cool you are. It's you sharing yourself with and getting to know dozens and then perhaps hundreds of people. Those people in turn mention you to their friends.

Before you know it, the multiplying effect takes hold and thousands of people are hearing about you and responding.

The thing is, no one message or comment or blog post or bulletin puts you over the top. It's the combined effect of all your networking efforts that builds over time. It is drops in a bucket that turn into a steady trickle and, before you know it, a full-blown waterfall that erupts into a tidal wave.

Now get busy turning on your MySpace friend and fan faucet!

Printed in the United States
71153LV00002B/58-60